EXPLORERS & DISCOVERERS

EXPLORERS & DISCOVERERS

From Alexander the Great to Sally Ride

Volume
Po-Z

Peggy Saari
•
Daniel B. Baker

AN IMPRINT OF GALE RESEARCH INC.,
AN INTERNATIONAL THOMPSON PUBLISHING COMPANY

NEW YORK • LONDON • BONN • BOSTON • DETROIT • MADRID
MELBOURNE • MEXICO CITY • PARIS • SINGAPORE • TOKYO
TORONTO • WASHINGTON • ALBANY NY • BELMONT CA • CINCINNATI OH

Explorers and Discoverers

From Alexander the Great to Sally Ride

Peggy Saari and Daniel B. Baker

Staff

Carol DeKane Nagel, *U·X·L Developmental Editor*
Thomas L. Romig, *U·X·L Publisher*

Shanna Heilveil, *Production Associate*
Evi Seoud, *Assistant Production Manager*
Mary Beth Trimper, *Production Director*

Pamela A. E. Galbreath, *Page and Cover Designer*
Cynthia Baldwin, *Art Director*

Margaret A. Chamberlain, *Permissions Supervisor (Pictures)*

The Graphix Group, *Typesetter*

∞™ This book is printed on acid-free paper that meets the minimum requirements of American National Standard for Information Sciences—Permanence Paper for Printed Library Materials, ANSI Z39.48-1984.

ISBN 0-8103-9787-8 (Set)
ISBN 0-8103-9798-6 (Volume 1)
ISBN 0-8103-9799-4 (Volume 2)
ISBN 0-8103-9800-1 (Volume 3)
ISBN 0-8103-9801-X (Volume 4)

Printed in the United States of America

Published simultaneously in the United Kingdom
by Gale Research International Limited
(An affiliated company of Gale Research Inc.)

I(T)P™   U•X•L is an imprint of Gale Research Inc.,
an International Thomson Publishing Company.
ITP logo is a trademark under license.

Contents

Biographical Listings

Volume 1: A-Ca

Volume 3: Hi-Pi

Preface

Explorers and Discoverers: From Alexander the Great to Sally Ride features biographies of 171 men, women, and machines who have expanded the horizons of our world and universe. Beginning with ancient Greek scholars and travelers and extending to twentieth-century oceanographers and astronauts, *Explorers and Discoverers* tells of the lives and times of both well-known and lesser-known explorers and includes many women and non-European explorers whose contributions have often been overlooked in the past. Who these travelers were, when and how they lived and traveled, why their journeys were significant, and what the consequences of their discoveries were are all answered within these biographies.

The 160 biographical entries of *Explorers and Discoverers* are arranged in alphabetical order over four volumes. Because the paths of these explorers often crossed, an entry about one explorer may refer to other explorers whose biographies also appear in *Explorers and Discoverers*. When this occurs, the other explorers' names appear in bold letters and are followed by a parenthetical note to see the appropriate entry for further information. The 176 illustrations and maps bring the subjects to life as well as provide geographic details of specific journeys. Additionally, 16 maps of major regions of the world lead off each volume, and each volume concludes with a chronology of exploration by region, a list of explorers by place of birth, and an extensive cumulative index.

Comments and Suggestions

We welcome your comments on this work as well as your suggestions for individuals to be featured in future editions of *Explorers and Discoverers*. Please write: Editors, *Explorers and Discoverers*, U·X·L, 835 Penobscot Bldg., Detroit, Michigan 48226-4094; call toll-free: 1-800-877-4253; or fax: 313-961-6348.

Introduction

Explorers and Discoverers: From Alexander the Great to Sally Ride takes the reader on an adventure with 171 men and women who have made significant contributions to human knowledge of the earth and the universe. Journeying through the centuries from ancient times to the present, we will conquer frontiers and sail uncharted waters. We will trek across treacherous mountains, scorching deserts, steamy jungles, and icy glaciers. We will plumb the depths of the oceans, land on the moon, and test the limits of outer space. Encountering isolation, disease, and even death, we will experience the exhilaration of triumph and the desolation of defeat.

Before joining the explorers and discoverers, however, it is worthwhile to consider why they venture into the unknown. Certainly a primary motivation is curiosity: they want to find out what is on the other side of a mountain, or they are intrigued by rumors about a strange new land, or they simply enjoy wandering the world. Yet adventurers often—indeed, usually—embark on a journey of discovery under less spontaneous circumstances; many of the great explorers were commissioned to lead an expedition with a specific mission. For instance, Spanish and Portuguese states sent **Christopher Columbus, Vasco da Gama,** and the sixteenth-century *conquistadors* on voyages to the New World in search of wealth.

Explorers also receive support from private investors. Prince **Henry the Navigator** financed expeditions along the coast of Africa. The popes of Rome sent emissaries to the Mongol khans. The Hudson's Bay Company, through the development of fur trade, was largely responsible for the exploration of Canada. **Joseph Banks** and the Royal Geographical Society backed the great nineteenth-century expeditions to the African continent. In each of these cases the explorer's discoveries resulted in lucrative trade routes and increased political power for the investor's home country.

Religion has been another strong motivating force for exploration. Famous Chinese travelers such as **Hsüang-tsang,** who was a Buddhist monk, went to India to obtain sacred Buddhist texts. **Abu Abdallah Ibn Battutah,** a Muslim, explored the Islamic world during a pilgrimage to Mecca. The medieval travel writer and rabbi **Benjamin of Tudela** investigated the state of Jewish communities throughout the Holy Land. Later, Christian missionaries **Johann Ludwig Krapf, Annie Royle Taylor,** and **Susie Carson Rijnhart** took their faith to the indigenous peoples of Asia and Africa.

Explorers have been inspired, too, by the quest for knowledge about the world. **Alexander von Humboldt** made an expedition to South America that collected a wealth of scientific information, while **James Cook** is credited with having done more than any other explorer to increase human knowledge of world geography. **Charles Darwin**'s famous voyage to South America aboard the Beagle resulted in his revolutionary theory of evolution.

Perhaps the foremost motivation to explore, however, is the desire to be the first to accomplish a particular feat. For instance, for nearly three centuries European nations engaged in a competition to be the first to find the Northwest Passage, a water route between the Atlantic and Pacific oceans, which the Norwegian explorer **Roald Amundsen** successfully navigated in 1903. Similarly, in the 1950s the United States and the Soviet Union became involved in a "space race," which culminated in 1969 when **Neil Armstrong** became the first human to walk on the moon.

Sometimes the spirit of cooperation can also be an incentive. During an 18-month period of maximum sunspot activity, from July 1957 through December 1958, 67 nations joined together to study the solar-terrestrial environment. Known as the International Geophysical Year, the project resulted in several major scientific discoveries along with the setting aside of Antarctica as a region for purposes of nonmilitary, international scientific research.

Although daring individuals throughout history have been driven by the desire to be first, the achievement began to take on special meaning with the increasing participation of women in travel and exploration during the nineteenth century. Pioneering women such as **Hester Stanhope, Mary Kingsley,** and **Alexandra David-Neel** broke away from rigid social roles to make remarkable journeys, but their accomplishments have only recently received the recognition they deserve. Since the advent of the aviation age in the early twentieth century, however, women have truly been at the forefront of exploration. **Amelia Earhart, Amy Johnson,** and **Beryl Markham** achieved as many flying "firsts" as their male colleagues; Soviet cosmonaut **Valentina Tereshkova** and U.S. astronaut **Sally Ride,** the first women in space, have made important contributions to space exploration.

By concentrating on biographies of individual explorers in this book we seem to suggest that these adventurers were loners who set out on their own to singlehandedly confront the unknown. Yet possibly the only "one-man show" was **René Caillié,** the first Westerner to travel to the forbidden city of Timbuktu and return alive. As a rule, explorers rarely traveled alone and they had help in achieving their goals. Therefore, use of an individual name is often only shorthand for the achievements of the expedition as a whole.

Famous explorers of Africa like **Richard Burton, John Hanning Speke, David Livingstone,** and **Henry Morton Stanley,** for instance, were all accompanied by large groups of servants and porters. In fact, the freed African slave **James Chuma,** who was the caravan leader for Livingstone and several other explorers, has been credited with the success of more than one expedition. Similar stories occur in other areas of exploration. For example, **Robert Edwin Peary** is considered to be the first person to reach the North Pole, yet he was accompanied by **Matthew A. Henson,** his African American assistant, and four Inuit—Egingwah, Seeglo, Ootah, and Ooqueah.

Explorers and Discoverers tells the stories of these men and women as well as others motivated by a daring spirit and an intense curiosity. They ventured forth to rediscover remote lands, to conquer the last frontiers, and to increase our knowledge of the world and the universe.

A final note of clarification: When we say that an explorer "discovered" a place, we do not mean she or he was the first human ever to have been there. Although the discoverer may have been the first from his or her country to set foot in a new land, most areas of the world during the great periods of exploration were already occupied or their existence had been verified by other people.

Picture Credits

The photographs and illustrations appearing in *Explorers and Discoverers: From Alexander the Great to Sally Ride* were received from the following sources:

On the cover: John Smith; **The Granger Collection, New York:** Beryl Markham and Matthew A. Henson.

UPI/Bettmann: pages 1, 129, 306, 375, 406, 489, 555, 611, 657, 699, 733, 742, 817, 856; **Norwegian Information Service:** page 14; **NASA:** pages 26, 30, 31, 34, 351, 400, 588, 723, 779, 844, 847; **The Granger Collection, New York:** pages 43, 44, 52, 61, 81, 86, 107, 122, 133, 141, 144, 145, 150, 164, 179, 187, 193, 209, 225, 282, 285, 311, 321, 325, 330, 334, 336, 345, 355, 359, 393, 424, 428, 433, 449, 460, 474, 499, 508, 512, 524, 560, 578, 589, 632, 638, 704, 744, 757, 772, 783, 806, 811, 830, 836, 852, 864; **The Bettmann Archive:** pages 169, 176, 268, 303, 341, 464, 494, 528, 623, 653, 695, 735, 767, 809, 828, 867; **Novosti Press Agency, Moscow:** page 378; **Hulton Deutsch Collection Limited:** page 418; **AP/Wide World Photos:** pages 538, 800;

Maps

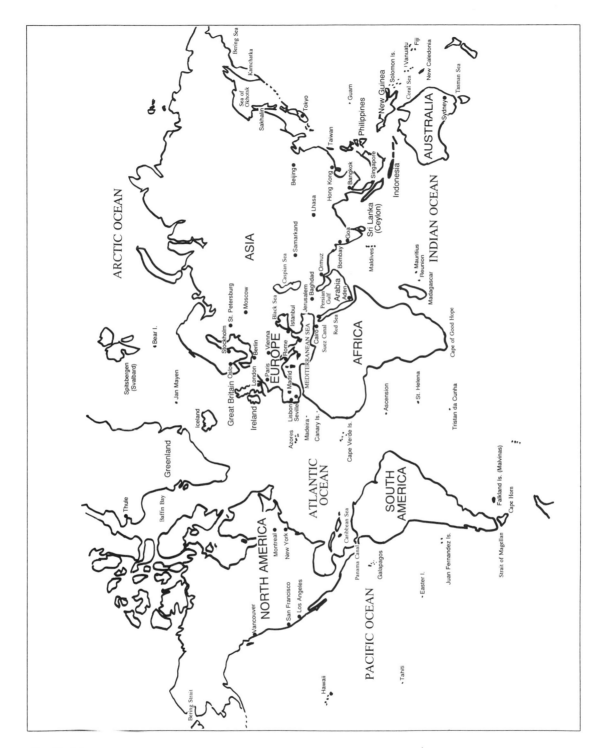

The World

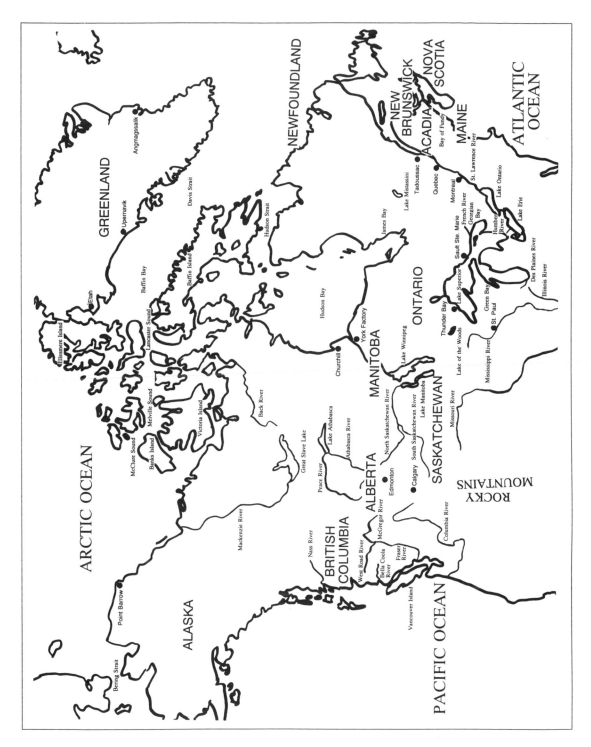

Americas—Canada.

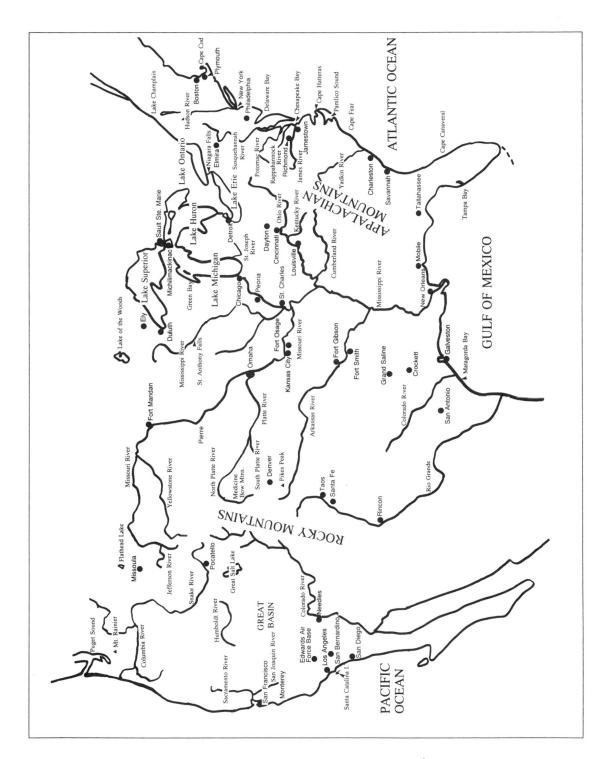

Americas—United States of America.

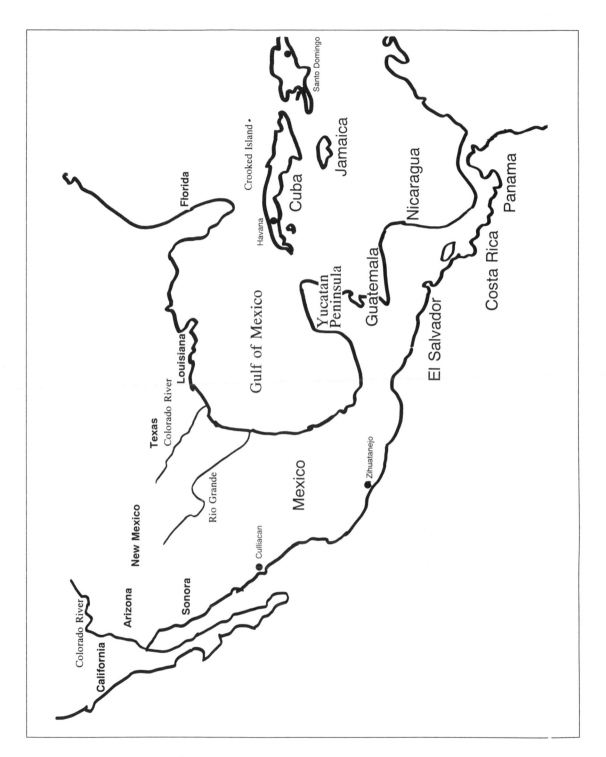

Florida

Crooked Island •

Santo Domingo

Cuba

Havana

Jamaica

Nicaragua

Panama

Gulf of Mexico

Yucatan Peninsula

Guatemala

El Salvador

Costa Rica

Louisiana

Texas

Colorado River

New Mexico

Rio Grande

Mexico

Zihuatanejo

Culliacan

Arizona

Sonora

Colorado River

California

Americas–Mexico and Central America.

Americas–South America.

Africa and the Middle East—Northwest Africa.

Africa and the Middle East—The Middle East and Arabia.

Africa and the Middle East—Eastern Africa.

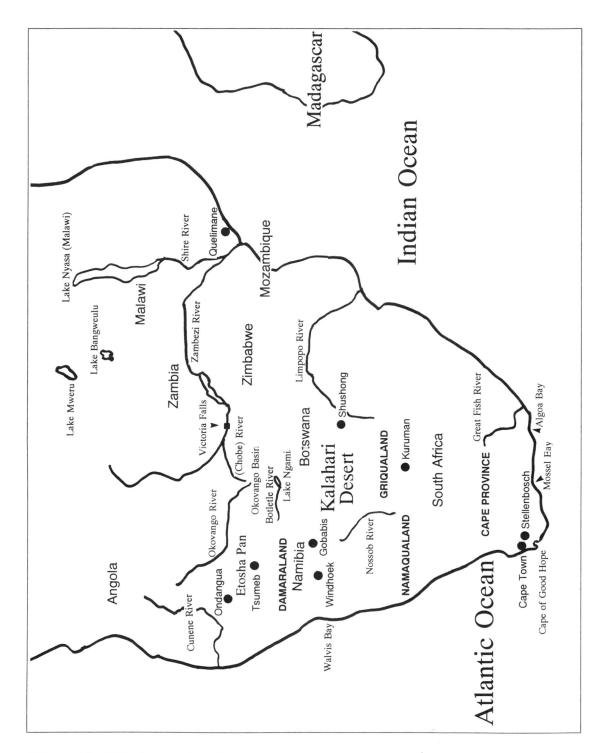

Africa and the Middle East—Southern Africa.

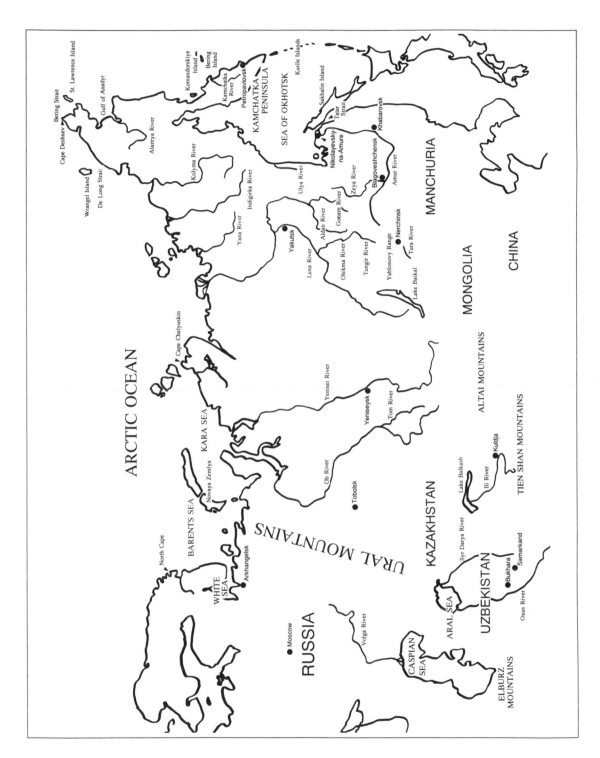

Asia—Siberia.

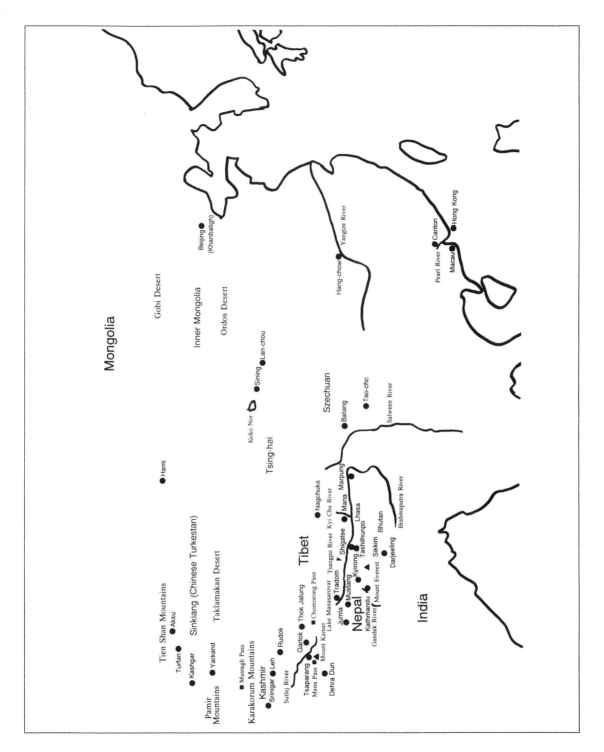

Asia—China and Tibet.

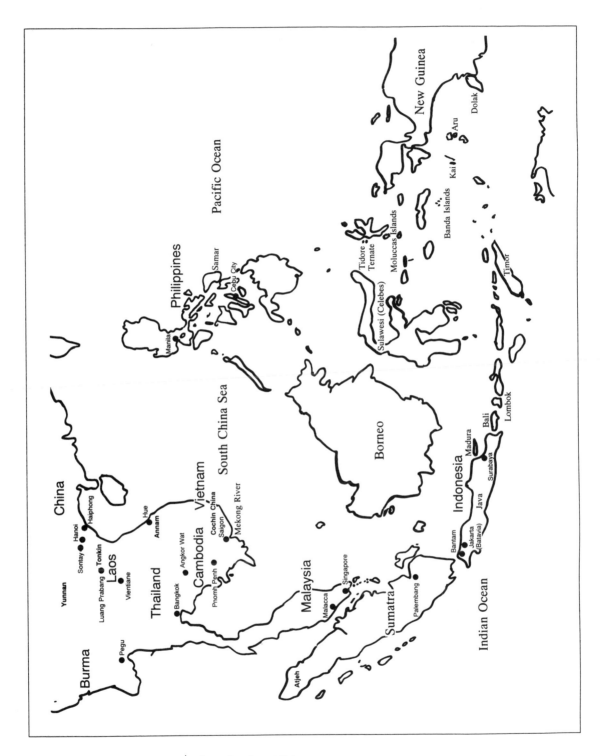

Asia—Southeast Asia.

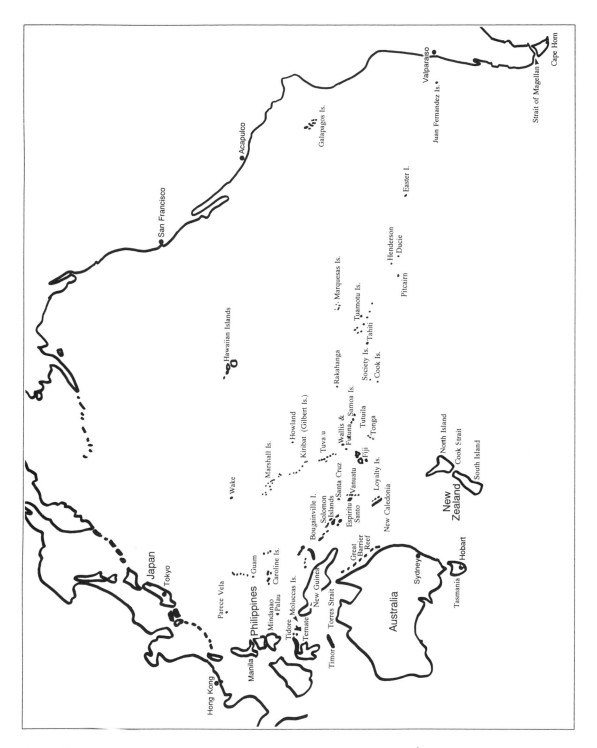

Pacific Ocean—Oceanea.

Pacific Ocean—Australia.

Arctic Region.

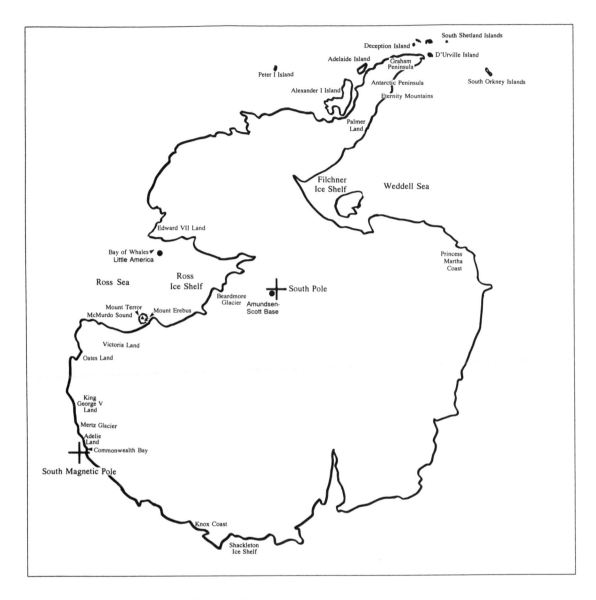

Antarctic Region.

EXPLORERS & DISCOVERERS

Marco Polo

Born 1254,
Venice, Italy

Died 1324,
Venice, Italy

I n the *Book of Ser Marco Polo,* Marco Polo described in detail each region he passed through during his 24-year journey in Asia; he also gave accounts based on hearsay of places he did not visit. European readers of his day regarded Polo's stories as fictional because they described regions and cultures that were completely foreign to Europeans. Scholars have accepted his material as accurate, however, and until the nineteenth century Polo's book was virtually the only source of information about Asia for Westerners.

In 1253 Niccolò and Maffeo Polo, two brothers from Venice, Italy, went on a trading expedition to Constantinople, which is now the city of Istanbul, in Turkey. When they were ready to return to Venice their route was blocked by a war, so they made a detour through K'ai-feng in China, the eastern capital of the Mongol emperor Kublai Khan, who had conquered China and most of Asia. The Polos reached Venice in 1269. While they were away, Niccolò's wife died and his son Marco was born and had reached the age of 15. The brothers

Marco Polo was an Italian who made an overland journey to China in the thirteenth century and became a friend of Mongol emperor Kublai Khan; Polo lived and traveled in Asia for 24 years.

Niccolò Polo and Maffeo Polo

Niccolò and Maffeo Polo were and younger sons of Andrea Polo, a nobleman of the San Felice quarter of Venice. The third son, Marco, gave his name to Niccolò's oldest son. In 1253 Niccolò and Maffeo set out on a trading voyage to Constantinople, the Greek capital of the Eastern Roman Empire. In 1260 the two Venetian merchants decided to move their operations to the Crimean port of Sudak, where there was already a Venetian colony and where the Polo family seems to have had trading interests. There they specialized in trading in precious stones. In order to expand their trade with the Mongol Empire they traveled to Sarai, the headquarters of the Mongol leader Barka Khan on the Volga River, and to Bolgara, another town farther north on the Volga. In 1262 they proposed to return to Venice but war broke out between Barka and Hulagu Khan, his cousin and the brother of Kublai Khan. By this time, Niccolò and Maffeo spoke the Mongol language quite well, and they decided to travel east through the Mongol lands, hoping to find a roundabout way to get back home. Because the routes west were still cut off by war, the Polos were forced to stay three years in Bukhara.

While the Polo brothers were in Bukhara, an envoy from Kublai Khan to Hulagu Khan passed through the city on his way back to Kublai's court; when he met Niccolò and Maffeo he invited them to go with him. Kublai Khan gave the Polos a warm reception. He was especially interested in reports about the Christian religion and the head of its western branch, the pope of Rome. He offered to send them back to Italy as his representatives to the pope. They accepted quickly because they understood that as the Great Khan's envoys, carrying a tablet of gold bearing his seal, they would have no trouble in crossing Asia. Kublai gave them a letter to the pope requesting that he send 100 Christian scholars to train his court in their knowledge. He also requested some of the oil that burned above the tomb of Christ in Jerusalem.

In 1271, the Polos set out once again for the East, this time taking Marco with them. Their story then becomes part of the narrative that Marco told in his famous book. When Marco returned from his period of captivity in Genoa in August 1299, Niccolò still seems to have been alive; according to one account he may have died in 1300. Maffeo Polo seems to have died sometime after 1309 and before 1315.

were planning another trip to Kublai Khan's court in Khanbalik, which is now Beijing, China; this time they would take young Marco with them.

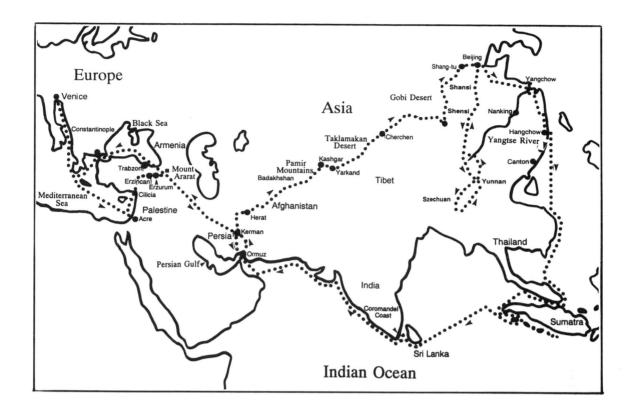

Goes with father and uncle to China

In 1271 the Polos left for the East. Although Kublai Khan's religion was Tibetan Buddhism, he had asked the Polo brothers to bring on their return visit some holy oil blessed by the pope. At the time the Polos were preparing to leave Italy the papacy was vacant, so they were unable to obtain any oil. The Polos planned to go to the port of Hormuz on the Persian Gulf, where they could take a ship to the East. On their way, they stopped in Palestine to meet with a Roman Catholic official named Teobaldo Visconti of Piacenza, who gave them letters for the Mongol emperor. Continuing their journey, the Polos soon learned that Teobaldo had been elected pope. They returned to Palestine so he could give them his blessing and the holy oil for Kublai.

From Palestine the Polos traveled north and east into Armenia. They passed near Mount Ararat, where Noah's ark is said to have landed, in what is today eastern Turkey. One of

During their travels throughout China and southeast Asia, Marco, Niccolò, and Maffeo Polo visited most of the important cities of the Eastern world.

the few personal stories in Marco Polo's book tells how, on the way to Hormuz, the Polos were attacked by bandits. They narrowly avoided capture by seeking refuge in a walled village nearby. Having made their escape, the Italians reached Hormuz safely. This port was a major center for trade with the East, and merchants from all over Europe and Asia could be found here. Polo would later describe in his book the bustling scene they encountered.

Becomes ill in Afghanistan

The Polos changed their plans to travel by sea when they saw the ships at Hormuz: these vessels looked so flimsy that the Italians decided to make the journey overland instead. The Polos traveled north through Persia, which is today known as Iran, to the city of Herat in Afghanistan. In Badakhshan, Afghanistan, Marco became ill. In his book he commented, "In those parts I had been ill for about a year, but on visiting the plateau [of Badakhshan] I recovered at once." It is not clear whether Marco's illness delayed the party for a year and, if so, where they stayed during that time, but their entire journey took three and a half years, which is much longer than is needed to travel the distance between Italy and China.

After leaving Badakhshan, the Polos began the ascent of the Pamir Plateau, which Marco said was "so high that it is said that it is the highest place in the world." At this point in the tale of his journey, Polo remarked that because the mountains were so cold it was hard to cook food. It is indeed more difficult to cook at high altitudes, but not because of the cold: the reason is that the lower atmospheric pressure causes water to boil at a lower temperature, and food therefore takes longer to cook.

Crosses Gobi Desert

Having traveled for 40 days over the plateau, the Polos had crossed into China. They descended to the city of Kashgar where Marco noted there were gardens and farms that grew grapes and cotton. They skirted the Takla Makan desert, passing through Yarkand, Khotan, and Cherchen to a city Polo called Lop, on the edge of the Gobi Desert. Lop was a resting place where travelers prepared for the desert crossing. It was necessary to carry a month's provisions in order to make the trip across the Gobi; fortunately water was available at locations 24 hours' journey apart. The trip was nonetheless hazardous, and Polo was told that the desert was inhabited by spirits who would call out to any traveler who was foolish enough to linger there. It took the Italians 30 days to cross the Gobi, a distance of about 300 miles.

Reaches Kublai Khan's court

Their next stop was the town of Tun-huang, which was a center of Buddhism in China. Then the caravan route headed to the southeast, paralleling the Great Wall of China, to Lanchou. Curiously, Polo did not mention the Great Wall, which he must have seen on this trip. The men followed the course of the Yellow River into the heartland of China.

At this point in their journey the Italians were met by emissaries from Kublai Khan and taken by horseback to meet the emperor. Kublai was staying at his summer capital at Shang-tu, or Xanadu, 300 miles north of Khanbalik. The Polos reached the court of the Great Khan in May 1275. The emperor was pleased to see his Italian friends; he was particularly happy to receive their gift of holy oil, which he seems to have assumed had magical qualities.

Becomes favorite of the khan

Kublai Khan became very fond of Marco, who was to serve the emperor in several ways in the following years. Likewise, Polo was a great admirer of Kublai, and believed that he was "the greatest Lord that is now in the world or ever has been." In his book, Polo describes the khan and gives a picture of life in his court, including a description of the palace at Shang-tu, which was the site of the Mongol capital during the summer months each year.

The Polos went with the khan when he traveled back to Khanbalik at the end of the season. Marco was even more impressed with the Mongol capital, with its wide avenues and famous Forbidden City, a walled area containing the imperial palaces. Each of Kublai's four wives maintained a separate court with 40,000 attendants. Polo described a magnificent banquet attended by 6,000 guests: "I will say nothing of the dishes, because you can readily imagine that there were a great many of every possible kind."

Becomes government official

After their arrival in Khanbalik, Niccolò and Maffeo went into the trading business. For his part, Marco became an official in Kublai's government. At the time, the government was in the hands of a corrupt official, who was killed in a conspiracy. At the inquest, Polo testified about the man's misdeeds, thus gaining him the trust of the khan. Kublai sent Polo on a trip to the province of Yunnan in southwestern China. He went through Sian, which had once been the capital of China, then crossed the provinces of Shensi and Szechwan before reaching K'un-ming, the Yunnan capital. It was on this trip that he passed near the borders of Tibet. Polo would later be the first European to write about that remote country.

Appointed governor of Yang-chou

For three years Polo served as the governor of the city of Yang-chou in the Kiangsu province not far from the former capital of Nanking on the Yang-tse River. During this time he traveled to Hangchow, a port south of modern Shanghai. This city had been the capital of the Southern Sung dynasty from 1135 until its capture by Kublai Khan in 1270. It probably had a population of about one and a half million at the time of Polo's visit. According to his account, it was "the finest and most splendid city in the world." Modern scholars consider this evaluation to have been accurate.

During the period that Polo was employed by Kublai, he traveled by sea to India, probably between 1284 and 1285. Along the way he visited the Kingdom of Champa in what is now Vietnam, and made stops in Thailand, Malaya, and Sumatra. From Sumatra he sailed to the Andaman Islands in the Bay of Bengal, and then to Sri Lanka.

Visits Sri Lanka

The purpose of Polo's visit to Sri Lanka may have been to obtain a major relic of the Buddhist religion—the tooth of Buddha—for Kublai. The Sri Lankans were willing to sell that and other religious objects at an enormous price, and the Mongols took the relics home to the khan. The east coast of India was Polo's next destination. Describing the practices of the Hindus he saw there, he wrote about the yogis who "fast all the year round and never drink anything but water." They slept naked on the ground, with no covering at all.

Settles in China

Polo returned to Khanbalik in about 1287. He and his father and uncle lived in China for many years. Eventually they thought of returning to Europe. Niccolò and Maffeo were by this time elderly men and must have felt that if they delayed their return too long they might not live to see their native city again. But Kublai Khan was reluctant to let his European friends go. "He was so fond of them," wrote Polo, "and so much enjoyed their company that nothing would induce him to give them leave."

In 1289 a message arrived from Kublai Khan's nephew, the Il-Khan, who ruled Persia. He wanted to marry and requested that Kublai send him a princess to be his bride. Kublai agreed to the request, and the Polos were able to persuade the khan to let them escort Princess Kokachin to her new home. They set sail for Hormuz with 14 ships in January 1292. The voyage became a two-year ordeal during which all but 18 of the 600 passengers and crew perished.

Returns home via Persia

Upon their arrival in Hormuz the Polos learned that Kublai Khan had died since they left China. Fortunately the

Italians had the khan's letters for their safe conduct home, as well as messages for the pope and the Christian kings of Europe. So the travelers were able to continue their journey through the interior safely. They rode north to Trabzon on the Black Sea in Asia Minor and from there to Constantinople. They reached Venice in 1295, after an absence of 24 years.

Recounts adventures while in captivity

Since the Polos were a family of merchants, Polo returned to this occupation once he was back in Venice. Eventually marrying and having several children, he worked as a merchant for the rest of his life. Polo did not write about his marvelous adventures himself. His story came to be written down only because of a fortunate meeting under less than fortunate circumstances. At the time of Polo's return from China there was great rivalry between the Italian ports of Venice and Genoa. In 1298 Marco was on board a ship that was captured by forces from Genoa. He was taken to that city and put into prison, where he met an Italian writer named Rustichello. During his two years in captivity Polo recounted the story of his travels to Rustichello, who wrote the *Book of Ser Marco Polo*.

Polo intended the book as a factual, geographical picture of the East. Although it was an immediate popular success, readers were reluctant to believe Polo's stories and the descriptions he gave of life in China. For instance, they were unfamiliar with such things as coal, asbestos, and paper currency, which Polo said he had seen, so they looked upon his report as simply a collection of legends. Although readers of Polo's day could not believe the customs and events he described, modern scholars agree that his accounts were quite accurate. Inaccuracies occur only when Polo touches on events and places he had not actually witnessed. Because of Polo's encounter with Rustichello, the story of his remarkable experiences in China has been preserved for modern readers.

Juan Ponce de León

Born 1460,
Tierra de Campos Palencia, Spain

Died July 1521,
Havana, Cuba

J uan Ponce de León was born in the village of Tierra de Campos Palencia in Spain. As a boy he was a page in the royal court of Aragon; later he served in various military campaigns against the Muslims in southern Spain until, in 1492, they were driven out of Granada. After sailing with **Christopher Columbus** (see entry) in 1493 on his second voyage to the New World, Ponce de León remained in Santo Domingo, which is the present-day Dominican Republic.

Juan Ponce de León, a Spanish soldier and explorer, was the first European to visit Florida.

Founds oldest settlement

In 1504 Ponce de León took part in a campaign against Native Americans in the Dominican province of Higüey in the northern part of the island. As a reward for Ponce de León's role in suppressing an insurrection, the governor of Hispaniola named him provincial governor of the eastern part of Hispaniola. In 1508 a Native American from the neighboring island of Borinquen, which was later named Puerto Rico by the

Spanish, arrived in Santo Domingo with a large nugget of gold. Since Europeans were always interested in gold, Ponce de León led an expedition to Puerto Rico. After finding traces of gold, he returned to the island in 1509 with settlers and founded Capara, the colony's oldest settlement, near present-day San Juan. Following his conquest Ponce de León was named governor of the new Spanish possession.

During the takeover of Puerto Rico, Ponce de León had been so ruthless in his treatment of the Native Americans that reports of his behavior were sent back to Spain. He was removed from office when Columbus's son Diego was confirmed as Spanish viceroy in the Caribbean with the power to make all appointments. By the time Ponce de León left Puerto Rico, however, he was a wealthy man.

Discovers Florida

In order to make up for his loss, Ponce de León was given the right to find and take possession of Bimini, which is today one of the islands in the Bahamas. In the early sixteenth century it was the name for a vague region north of Santo Domingo and Cuba that contained "the fountain of youth." According to myth, anyone who drank from the fountain would have eternal youth. Ponce de León is generally believed to have organized an expedition at his own expense for the purpose of finding the fountain; however, many historians contend that he was more interested in the tales of wealth in the new land.

Whatever his intent, Ponce de León left the port of San Germain, Puerto Rico, with three ships in March 1513. They sailed northwest, stopping at Grand Turk Island and then at San Salvador, the first place sighted by Columbus, where they stayed for a few days. They continued sailing northwest until they sighted land on April 2, which was Palm Sunday. Ponce de León landed on the mainland of North America, near the site of modern-day St. Augustine, Florida; at the time he did not realize he had landed on the continent, instead thinking he had found an island. He named the new land Florida, perhaps because of the flowers he saw—*florida* means flowery in

Spanish—or as a remembrance of Easter, which is *la pascua florida* in Spanish. The next day Ponce de León took possession of Florida in the name of the king of Spain.

Discovers Gulf Stream

On April 8 Ponce de León and his party sailed south; however, they were slowed down by a heavy current, the Gulf Stream, which Ponce de León is credited with discovering and which opened a new route for travel from Spain to North America. As the Spaniards were sailing along the shore some Native Americans signaled for them to land; as the party came ashore the Native Americans tried to take their boat. Fighting erupted, and two Spaniards were wounded. Farther south, at a place called Santa Cruz, which is now probably Jupiter Inlet, Ponce de León seized a Native American as a hostage who also served as pilot.

Still searching for Bimini, the Spanish ships sailed through the Florida Keys and the Dry Tortugas to Cuba and back to Florida. Having no luck, they sailed back to Spain via the Bahamas; one of the ships went off to continue the search for Bimini and found Andros Island.

Resumes search for Bimini

Ponce de León returned to Puerto Rico, where he once again became involved in putting down Native American rebellions. After order had been restored he went back to Spain to report on his Florida expedition to King Ferdinand. The king named him captain-general in September 1514 and commissioned him to continue the search for Bimini. On his return to the Caribbean, Ponce de León led an unsuccessful campaign against the Caribs in the islands south of Puerto Rico. He remained in Puerto Rico for five years before leaving on a voyage to find Bimini.

Ponce de León left Puerto Rico in February 1521 with two ships and 200 men. The party landed on the west coast of Florida, probably near present-day Charlotte Harbor. When they went ashore they were met by a large force of Native

Americans who shot a volley of arrows at the intruders. Hit by one of the arrows, Ponce de León was taken aboard the flagship and transported to Cuba. When he died in July 1521 he was buried under the main altar of the Dominican church in San Juan, Puerto Rico. The inscription on his tomb reads: "Beneath this stone repose the bones of the valiant Lion [the *León* in his name means "lion"] whose deeds surpassed the greatness of his name."

Wiley Post

Born 1899,
Grand Saline, Texas

Died August 15, 1935,
Point Barrow, Alaska

After learning to fly by working as a stuntman in an air show, Wiley Post went on to set a speed record for flying around the world. This American aviator then became the first person to fly solo around the globe. If an accident had not cut short his life, Post might well have gone on to other major achievements in aviation.

Post grew up on farms in Texas and Oklahoma. He quit school after the eighth grade to work at odd jobs. He had decided at an early age that he wanted to be an aviator, but he had a problem finding the money for flying lessons. As it turned out, his courage helped him find a way to overcome this obstacle.

Pursues interest in flying

Post was in Texas in 1924 when he went to see pilots do stunts in a "flying circus." The circus parachute jumper was injured and could not perform. Although he had been in a

Wiley Post was an American aviator who set a speed record for flying around the world; he later became the first person to fly solo around the world.

plane only once—and had never jumped out of one—he volunteered to substitute for the parachutist. At 2,000 feet he climbed out onto the right wing and jumped off. Impressed, the circus owners hired him, and thus Post began his career in aviation by making 99 parachute jumps. Living and working with the pilots, he picked up some flying instruction and with a little more training made his first solo flight in 1926.

In order to pay for his flight training, Post was also working as a driller on an oil field. One day there was an accident at the rig and a bolt flew up, striking Post in the left eye; the eye eventually had to be removed. Not to be discouraged, Post trained himself to see almost as well as before so that he could keep flying. With the worker's compensation money that he got for his injury, Post bought his first airplane. He soon wrecked the plane, but he had only begun his flying career.

Works as pilot

In 1927 Post took a job as pilot for Oklahoma oilman F. C. Hall. Three years later he flew Hall's plane to victory in the Los Angeles-Chicago Bendix Trophy Race in 1930. The $7,500 prize money they gained led Post and Hall to start thinking about other record-breaking flights they might make with the *Winnie Mae,* as Hall's plane was called.

Their ambitious plan was to break the speed record for flying around the world. Post took the *Winnie Mae* to California and worked with navigator Harold Gatty in mapping out a route. They made modifications to the plane, and Post worked to get himself in physical condition for a long-range flight. As he wrote later in a book titled *Around the World in Eight Days,* "I knew that the variance in time as we progressed would bring on acute fatigue if I were used to regular hours." Post seems to have been the first person to appreciate the effects of jet lag.

Sets out to break record

After obtaining permission from the governments of countries they would fly over, Post and Gatty took off, leaving

New York at 4:55 A.M. on June 23, 1931. They landed first in Newfoundland. Their plan was to fly from there straight on to Germany, but after flying by instruments for 16 hours with no visibility they needed to make certain of their position. They dropped down and landed in a field in western England. Asked later about this stopover, Post joked, "I don't think we can honestly say we were lost ... we just didn't know where we were."

Post and Gatty flew on to Germany, again with no visibility, landing in the city of Hanover. They were so tired that after taking off they realized they had forgotten to check their fuel supply, so the *Winnie Mae* returned to Hanover to refuel. After finally reaching the German capital of Berlin, the aviators were able to get their first sleep in almost 35 hours.

The two Americans reached Moscow about eight hours after leaving Berlin. Next they flew along the route of the Trans-Siberian Railroad to Novosibirsk, Irkutsk, and Blagoveshchensk, where the plane got stuck in the mud and had to be pulled out by a detachment of Russian soldiers. They then flew to Khabarovsk, landing there on June 28; they were forced to wait for 12 hours before taking off again because of bad weather and engine repairs.

Encounters more problems

From Khabarovsk, Post and Gatty traveled all the way to Alaska, crossing the Sea of Okhotsk and the Bering Sea on their way to North America. This was the longest and most dangerous leg of the trip. With almost no gas left in their tanks they landed near Nome, Alaska, after a flight of 16 hours and 45 minutes.

When they were preparing to take off again, the plane nosed off the runway into soft sand and the propeller was damaged. As the two men worked on the propeller, the engine backfired, and the propeller hit Gatty, badly spraining his back. They made a three-hour flight to Fairbanks, Alaska, where Gatty could see a doctor and they could get a new propeller for the plane.

Post and Gatty flew through heavy rain over the Canadian Rockies, then landed at the airfield in Edmonton, Alberta.

The field had been turned to mud, so town officials agreed to let the plane take off from the main street of the city. While Post and Gatty slept, the townspeople took down all the electricity and telephone lines on Portage Avenue so that the *Winnie Mae* could take off.

Sets record and seeks new one

The next stop was Cleveland, Ohio. Then came the final leg of the flight, to New York City. The *Winnie Mae* touched down in New York on July 1, 1931. It had taken the pilots 8 days, 15 hours, and 51 minutes to circle the globe. Post's flight took 12 days off the previous record. Following his record-breaking flight he received an enormous amount of attention from the press and public. Post bought the *Winnie Mae* from Hall, and then set out looking for new financial backing so he could carry out his next exploit—flying around the world by himself.

During preparations for his solo flight, Post had a minor accident while taking some friends up in his plane. The fuel gauge read empty but Post insisted he had just filled the tanks. He did not know that some teenagers had siphoned off the gas for their car. The plane crashed, but no one was seriously injured. Post rebuilt the plane and made changes that helped it to fly better over long distances.

By 1933 Post had pulled together enough money to make his solo flight. His backing came from a group of businessmen and companies promoting the aviation business. He had equipped the *Winnie Mae* with one of the first automatic pilots. Without this technological advance Post's flight would have been impossible. Post planned to take almost exactly the same route as before but with fewer stops along the way. This was only possible because he had modified the plane and was flying without a passenger.

Becomes first to fly nonstop

Post took off from New York at 5:10 A.M. on July 15 and flew straight to Berlin in 25 hours and 45 minutes. He was the first person to fly that great distance nonstop. He was greeted in Berlin by a cheering crowd, and met Hermann Goering, the head of the German Luftwaffe, or air force.

Post left Berlin after an inadequate rest of only 2 hours and 15 minutes. He had to stop soon afterwards when he realized he had forgotten his maps. When the weather turned bad he stopped for six hours of much-needed sleep.

Because of persistent trouble with the automatic pilot, Post was forced to land many times as he crossed the Soviet Union. He had to stop in Moscow, Novosibirsk, Irkutsk, a village called Skovorodino, and Khabarovsk. From Khabarovsk, Post flew to Alaska, where a combination of radio problems, poor visibility, and fatigue combined to make him lose his way. After circling aimlessly for several hours he finally found a place to land at a small settlement called Flat in central Alaska. Since the runway was very short, the plane ran off into a ditch and bent the propeller. While Post slept, local volunteers salvaged the plane and a bush pilot flew in a new propeller from Fairbanks.

Sets solo record

From Alaska, Post flew to Edmonton and then on to Floyd Bennett Field in New York. A cheering crowd of 50,000 people was waiting to greet him. He had flown around the world in 7 days, 18 hours, and 49 minutes, beating his previous record by 21 hours. And he had done it alone. Post did not live to set new records. The first man to fly solo around the world was killed two years later in an accident with a friend, the humorist Will Rogers. Their plane crashed as they were flying near Point Barrow, Alaska.

Nikolay Przhevalsky

Born April 12, 1839,
Kimborovo, Russia

Died November 1, 1888,
Karakol (now Przhevalsk), Russia

Nikolay Przhevalsky was a Russian explorer who led five major expeditions to the Far East and central Asia.

During his lifetime Nikolay Mikhaylovich Przhevalsky gained considerable fame for his explorations in the Russian Far East, Mongolia, Sinkiang, and Tibet. He wrote books about his adventures, was honored by geographical societies throughout Europe, and even discovered a wild horse that was named after him. Yet Przhevalsky never realized his dream: to explore the "Forbidden Kingdom" of Tibet. He died during his last journey to that country.

After finishing high school, Przhevalsky joined the Russian army. He served during the Crimean War and then entered officer training school. While he was a student he wrote a paper on the Russian Far East that gained him membership in the St. Petersburg Imperial Geographical Society. In 1863, before his graduation, he was sent to Poland, which was still part of the Russian Empire, to help suppress a revolt. Following active duty he taught in a military academy in Warsaw for two years. In 1866 he was assigned to a base in eastern Siberia.

Leads expedition to central Asia

In 1868, soon after Przhevalsky's arrival in Siberia, he was sent to the Ussuri River, a tributary of the Amur, in the Russian Far East, to make a report on its geography and topography. When he submitted the report his superiors were so impressed with his work that he felt confident enough to seek permission to lead his own expedition to central Asia. In January 1870 he went to St. Petersburg to make a formal request to the army and to raise money for the trip. Although the main purpose of the expedition was scientific, Przhevalsky was able to get government support because he could explore regions that were important to Russia's strategic interests.

After making final preparations, Przhevalsky started out in August with a small group of Cossack guards. Their first stop was the town of Kyakhta on the Russian-Mongolian border. From there the Russian party traveled in rickety two-wheeled Chinese carts to Urga, which is now known as Ulan Bator, the capital of Mongolia. In Urga they joined a caravan headed for Kalgan, a Chinese city north of Beijing. They made a difficult winter crossing of the Gobi Desert, where temperatures dropped to -34°F at night.

Reaching Kalgan on May 7, 1871, the party made trips to Beijing, Dalai Nor (Great Lake), and the Ordos Desert in Inner Mongolia. Przhevalsky also intended to visit Koko Nor, a lake in the Tsinghai province, but he was running out of money and his companions were unwilling to go with him. So, just 400 miles short of his goal, he was forced to turn back. On the return trip their camels were stolen, but the expedition finally reached the Kalgan safely.

Tries to enter Tibet

In March 1872 Przhevalsky and several new companions set out for Koko Nor once again. This time they reached their destination; after visiting the lake they made a midsummer crossing of the Ordos Desert and moved southward across the salt plains of Tsaidam toward Tibet. Exploring this country, which was forbidden to Westerners, had become Przhevalsky's ultimate goal. Once again, however, he encountered problems. At the Dza-chu River (which is now called the Mekong) on the frontier between the Chinese province of Tsinghai and Tibet, he was forced to turn back. By now his camels had died and he had run out of money. Nonetheless, upon his return to Russia, Przhevalsky was promoted to lieutenant colonel and recognized for his travels with several awards.

Rediscovers Lop Nor

The explorer's next expedition, in 1876, would have a distinctly political motive. Because the ruler of one of the states between China and Russia seemed ready to transfer his allegiance to Russia, Przhevalsky was sent to negotiate with him. The meeting did not result in the changes the Russians desired, but after it was over the ruler did supply Przhevalsky with an escort to take him through the Sinkiang region of China. He explored this area and wrote descriptions of the Tien Shan range and the Tarim Basin.

Przhevalsky's major accomplishment on this trip occurred in December 1876 when he reached Lop Nor, which no European had visited since **Marco Polo** in the late thirteenth century (see entry). A shallow lake between the Turfan Depression and the Takla Makan Desert, Lop Nor has never been accurately described because, for reasons that are not understood, its location changes. As a result of his visit Przhevalsky advanced several theories to explain this phenomenon.

Leaving Lop Nor, Przhevalsky made an attempt to cross the Astin Tagh Mountains (now known as the A-erh-chin Shan-mo) but was forced to turn back. He traveled to Kuldja, a small town between the Tien Shan and the Ala Tau mountains, where he became ill. While recuperating he wrote an account of his expedition, titled *Mongolia and the Tangut Country*. A translation of another of his works, *Across the Tian Shan to Lop-Nor,* appeared in 1879.

Searches for the "Forbidden Kingdom"

Przhevalsky still had not visited Tibet. He was determined

to reach the "Forbidden Kingdom" on his next expedition, which took place in 1879. His starting point was the town of Zaysan, near the border between China and Russia, where he received an unusual but important gift. As he was about to depart he was presented with the skin of a wild horse. The existence of this type of horse had long been rumored but had never been confirmed by Europeans. Przhevalsky was credited with discovering the animal, which was later named "Przhevalsky's horse" in his honor; it is now known as Przewalski's horse.

From Zaysan, Przhevalsky traveled through Dzungaria north of the Tien Shan and over the Nan Shan before descending into the Tsaidam Depression. He then turned south into Tibet. He managed to cross the border, but at Nagchu, 170 miles from the Tibetan capital of Lhasa, Tibetan soldiers stopped him. Disappointed again, the explorer went back to Russia.

Discovers mountain ranges

Przhevalsky made another attempt to reach Tibet in August 1883. After assembling a party of 21 men, he went into Mongolia in November. While crossing the Gobi Desert they explored the headwaters of the Hwang Ho River. The men stopped at Koko Nor and then followed the southern margin of the Tsaidam Depression. In this area east of the Kun Lun Shan, Przhevalsky saw several mountain ranges that had never been reported on before. He named them after famous explorers; one range was later named in his honor.

Przewalski's horse

The only wild horse in existence that is not descended from a domestic horse, Przewalski's horse originated in an area that includes western Mongolia through northern Sinkiang in China. It is smaller than the average horse, with a large head and a protruding forehead. Grayish-brown in color, the horse has a dark, brush-like mane and a plume-like tail; a dark stripe runs down the middle of its back. Today Przewalski's horse can be found only in the Altai Mountains in western Mongolia, where herds migrate into the Gobi Desert each year; it is also bred in zoos.

The population of these wild horses has been reduced in modern times because they must share grazing land and water with domestic livestock. They have also bred with wild domestic horses, thus further decreasing the size of their herds. Experts speculate that even the horse Przhevalsky discovered may not have been a "pure" breed but rather a mixture, since the wild horse probably began to interbreed with Mongol horses several hundred years ago.

Przhevalsky led his party across the Astin Tagh range and spent two months investigating Lop Nor. He tried to turn south and enter Tibet, but once again Tibetan authorities prevented him from doing so. Changing his route, he skirted the southern part of the Takla Makan and went to the oasis and caravan town of Khotan. From Khotan he headed straight across the Takla Makan range, crossed the Tien Shan, and descended to Issyk Kul in Russia. He returned to St. Petersburg in January 1886.

Gains recognition throughout Europe

Przhevalsky's last expedition and his writings made him one of the most famous explorers at a time when explorers were major celebrities and heroes. He was promoted to major general and was given awards by geographical societies from all over Europe. Przhevalsky's fame did not satisfy him, however: he had not given up on his dream of visiting Lhasa. In the fall of 1888 he mounted what would be his final expedition. On his way to try for the last time to explore Tibet, Przhevalsky suddenly became ill. He died on November 1, 1888, near the Chinese border in the town of Karakol, which is today called Przhevalsk.

Pytheas

Born c. 380 B.C.,
Massalia, Gaul (France)

Died c. 300 B.C.,
Massalia, Gaul

P ytheas has generated more interest than any other of the ancient explorers. There are those who say that he is the first known explorer in the modern sense of the word. As a result, most histories of exploration have something to say about him. Pytheas was the first person to write about the British Isles and the Atlantic coast of Europe. His book, *On the Ocean,* has been lost, but the Greek historian Polybias left an account of his travels.

Sent to Britain

Pytheas was born around 380 B.C. in the Greek colony of Massalia, which is the present-day city of Marseilles, on the southern coast of France. Sometime toward the end of the fourth century B.C., he was sent out by the merchants of his native city to find a route to the tin mines of southern Britain, which provided that valuable metal for all of Europe and the Mediterranean. The trade in tin was controlled by the

Pytheas was a Greek navigator and geographer from the city of Massalia in southern France who traveled all the way around Britain; he also wrote the first account of Scandinavia.

Carthaginians, who lived in the area that is now Tunisia, and the Greeks wanted to break their monopoly.

At that time the Pillars of Hercules, or the Strait of Gibraltar, which is the passage from the Mediterranean into the Atlantic, was controlled by the Carthaginians. Pytheas reached the Atlantic either by going overland or by passing through the strait during a time of Carthaginian weakness, possibly when Carthage was fighting a war with Syracuse in Sicily. In any case, he reached the Phoenician city of Gades—now Cádiz, Spain—then followed the shoreline of Europe to the port of Corbilo at the mouth of the Loire River. From there he sailed to the island of Ouessant off the tip of Brittany.

Visits tin mines

Pytheas sailed from Brittany to Belerium, or Land's End, in Cornwall at the southwestern tip of Britain. There he visited the famous tin mines, which he described at length:

> The inhabitants of Britain who dwell about the headland of Belerium are unusually hospitable and have adopted a civilized manner of life because of their intercourse with foreign traders. It is they who work the tin, extracting it by an ingenious process. The bed itself is of rock but between are pieces of earth which they dig out to reach the tin. Then they work the tin into pieces the size of knuckle bones and carry it to an island that lies off Britain and is called Ictis [St. Michael's Mount, Cornwall]; for at the time of ebb tide the space between this island and the mainland becomes dry, and they can take the tin in large quantities over to the island on their wagons.

While Pytheas was in Britain he explored much of the island on foot and accurately estimated its circumference—4,000 miles—and he made a nearly correct calculation of the distance between northern Britain and Massalia—he estimated 1,050 miles and the actual distance is 1,120 miles.

Possibly reaches Scandinavia

From Cornwall, Pytheas sailed north through the Irish Sea between Britain and Ireland to the northern tip of Scotland, probably going as far as the Orkney Islands. Along the way, he stopped to travel short distances inland and described the customs of the inhabitants. Beyond northern Scotland, Pytheas found another land called the "Island of Thule."

According to Pytheas, Thule was a six-day journey north from Britain. In midsummer, the sun retires to its resting place for only two or three hours. The inhabitants lived on wild berries and "millet," or oats, and made a drink called mead from wild honey. From his description, Thule was probably Norway in the present region of the city of Trondheim, although other locations have been suggested. North of Thule he was told of a land where the sea became solid and the sun never set in summertime. These reports seemed so crazy to the people of the Mediterranean world that his report was not believed and was ridiculed for years afterward.

Ever since Pytheas's visit the far northern extremes of the earth have had the poetic name of Thule, which is also the name of the northernmost town in Greenland. It is not clear whether Pytheas actually went to Thule or merely reported what he had heard about it.

Goes home via Germany

Pytheas sailed back to Britain, then down its east coast and across the North Sea to the North Frisian Islands off the coast of Germany. Arriving at the island of Heligoland, which he called Abalus, he reported, "In the spring the waves wash up amber on the shores of this island. The inhabitants use it as fuel instead of wood ... and also sell it to their neighbors the Teutons." From there Pytheas sailed back along the coast of Europe and returned home.

Walter Raleigh

Born 1554,
Devon, England
Died October 29, 1618,
England

Sir Walter Raleigh was an English adventurer who sponsored the first attempted English settlement in North America; he led two expeditions to the Orinoco River in South America.

The dramatic course of Sir Walter Raleigh's life was repeatedly altered by tensions between England and Spain, the two great naval powers of the sixteenth century. His fortunes were also closely linked with Queen Elizabeth I. Raleigh attained a powerful position at court, but he regularly fell in and out of favor with the queen; once she even had him put in the Tower of London because he had secretly married one of her maids of honor. Raleigh was eventually sentenced to death for disobeying the orders of King James I, who succeeded to the throne after Elizabeth's death.

Walter Raleigh was born in the English county of Devon, the birthplace of many of England's famous navigators. In 1578 he sailed to North America with his half-brother Sir Humphrey Gilbert, who later founded the first permanent North American colony in New Zealand. This expedition was supposedly a "voyage of discovery," but historians believe Gilbert and Raleigh actually planned to attack and rob Spanish ships. Whatever their motive, they were forced to return to

England in 1579, without having reached the newly discovered continent, after their own ship was attacked by the Spanish.

Becomes queen's favorite

At the time of Raleigh's return from the unsuccessful voyage, the Irish, with the aid of Spain, were rebelling against English rule. Raleigh was immediately sent to the Munster province in Ireland, where he used cruel tactics against the Desmonds, who were leading the rebellion. When he returned to London in 1581 to deliver dispatches about the war, he caught the eye of Queen Elizabeth I. He soon became her "favorite" and, many assume, her lover. As a result of his connection with the queen Raleigh was showered with honors and he began to make a considerable amount of money through offices he held. He used his position to encourage English exploration and settlement in North America.

Supports settlement in North America

Raleigh supplied part of the money Gilbert needed for an expedition to Newfoundland in 1583. Raleigh wanted to go with Gilbert but was forbidden to do so by the queen; as it turned out, Gilbert died on the return voyage. Soon afterward, Raleigh received a "patent" for the coast of North America. This meant he had the exclusive right to explore and settle an area in the queen's name. In April 1584 he sent an expedition that was headed for the Caribbean and then sailed up along the coast of North America from Florida to North Carolina. The explorers claimed this area for England. On the return of the expedition the queen named the region Virginia, after herself—because she never married she was known as "the Virgin Queen."

In 1585 Raleigh was knighted and awarded vast estates in Ireland. Still interested in colonizing North America, he made plans to establish a permanent settlement in Virginia. Yet once again Elizabeth refused him permission to go to the new country himself. Instead he sent out a colonizing expedition under the command of his cousin, Sir Richard Grenville, in April 1585. The colonists occupied Roanoke Island off the coast of present-day North Carolina, but because they quarreled among themselves and with the Native Americans they encountered, their settlement failed; they were back in England just over a year later.

In the summer of 1587, the year he was appointed captain of the queen's guard, Raleigh sent a new expedition to Virginia under the command of John White. The party settled at Roanoke, the site of the colony that had failed two years earlier. Then White returned to England with the ships, leaving behind 89 men, 17 women, and two children in North America. The following spring Raleigh sent a ship full of supplies to the new colony, but on the way the ship was captured by the French. Around a year later, in 1589, Raleigh sent another relief expedition. By then it was too late: when the ships arrived in Virginia there was no trace of the settlement, which has since been known as "the lost colony." Raleigh lost £40,000 in the venture.

Imprisoned in Tower of London

In 1588 Raleigh was a member of the commission that planned England's defense against the Spanish Armada. At about this time he quarreled with the queen's new favorite, the earl of Essex, and lost some of his influence at court. In 1589 Raleigh left for Ireland, where he lived at Kilcolum Castle. During his stay he became the patron of Edmund Spenser, whose poem *The Faerie Queene* was a tribute to Elizabeth I. Raleigh is also credited with introducing the potato and tobacco into Ireland and England around this time. His influence with the queen continued to weaken, reaching its lowest point in 1592 when Elizabeth learned of his secret marriage to Elizabeth Throckmorton, a maid of honor at court. For this offense Raleigh was imprisoned in the Tower of London.

Raleigh was soon released from prison to handle a squabble among the members of an expedition he had sent to Portugal. When they came back in a ship loaded with riches, fights broke out over how the treasure should be divided. In exchange for his freedom Raleigh settled the dispute. Although he was still banned from court, he soon occupied himself with a new scheme. He had become fascinated by Spanish stories of a mythical place in South America called Manoa, which was supposed to be ruled by El Dorado, "the golden one." In 1593 Raleigh commissioned an expedition under Jacob Whiddon to explore the Orinoco River, which lies in modern-day Venezuela. Whiddon looked for Manoa but returned at the end of the year without having found the nonexistent country.

Searches for Manoa

Raleigh decided to go to South America himself. He left the English port of Plymouth on February 9, 1594, with a fleet of five ships. After six weeks his party arrived at the island of Trinidad; at the time Trinidad, which lies just off the north coast of South America, was ruled by the Spanish. Raleigh attacked and captured the town of San Jose. The town's governor showed him a letter written by a Spaniard, Juan Martinez, who claimed to have traveled up the Orinoco River and to have stayed in the fabulously wealthy country of Manoa.

The Englishmen set out to find Manoa themselves. Raleigh entered the Orinoco through its westernmost channel, the Manamo, and then rowed upstream with five of the ships' boats and 100 men. They traveled about 125 miles up the river to the point where the Caroni River flows into the Orinoco. By then the English were nearly out of supplies. There was, of course, no sign of the fabled country of Manoa.

Raleigh decided to leave two of the men with a group of Native Americans so they could learn the language in order to find out about Manoa. Then he returned with his party to Trinidad; after raiding several other Spanish settlements, Raleigh took his fleet back to England. Although they had little to show for their voyage, they did bring with them a load of ore that was later found to contain gold.

Regains favor at court

Raleigh's enemies in Queen Elizabeth's court continued to criticize him. He attempted to promote himself by writing a book titled *Discoverie of Guiana;* he also drew a map of the area he had explored. He sent another expedition to the Orinoco under the guidance of his friend Lawrence Kemys, who brought back news that the Spanish had established a fort near the mouth of the Caroni on the Orinoco.

In 1596 Raleigh commanded a squadron in an English assault on the Spanish port of Cádiz, where he was wounded and distinguished himself with his bravery. As a result, he was once more in the queen's favor; he returned to court in May 1597. In 1600 Raleigh was appointed governor of Jersey, one of the islands in the English Channel, where he stayed until the queen's death in 1603.

Lives in Tower for 13 years

When King James I ascended the throne, Raleigh's enemies convinced the king that Raleigh was guilty of treason—specifically of plotting to kill the king. Raleigh was stripped of all his offices and estates and sent to the Tower of London on July 17, 1603. Raleigh was so upset he tried to kill himself, but his attempt was unsuccessful. Convicted and sentenced to death, Raleigh was actually standing on the scaffold about to be beheaded when the news came that the king had changed his sentence to life imprisonment. For the next 13 years he lived with his wife and son in the Tower of London. During that time he wrote several books, including the first volume of his *History of the World,* which began with the year 160 B.C.

Returns to Guiana

In 1610 Raleigh began to argue in favor of sending another expedition to Guiana to look for gold. Six years later he was released from prison in order to lead an expedition, with orders not to attack any Spanish possessions or ships. Raleigh financed the expedition with his own money as well as with the investments of several friends. Leaving England in June 1617, the fleet of 14 ships immediately ran into a storm; many of the ships were damaged and one was sunk. They spent two months in an Irish port making repairs.

Throughout the voyage Raleigh's party encountered problems. Plagued by water shortages and storms, they were also becalmed and barely moved for 40 days. Then Raleigh and the crew became ill with fever; many of the men died. Finally they reached the coast of what is now French Guiana, where they were able to get fresh water and supplies. Raleigh then sent his friend Kemys up the Orinoco River with the majority of the men, including Raleigh's nephew and his son Walter. Raleigh stayed behind with the ships to guard against a Spanish attack.

Kemys violates king's order

Disregarding orders from the English king to leave the Spanish alone, Kemys and his men attacked San Tomás, the town the Spanish had established on the Orinoco. During the fighting Raleigh's son was killed. The defeated Spanish forces abandoned their town; Kemys did not pursue them through the heavy forest. When Kemys returned to the ships, Raleigh reproached him so severely that Kemys committed suicide.

Raleigh wanted to look for the rich mines he believed lay in the interior, but at this point none of his men would follow him. The ships separated and Raleigh sailed north to Newfoundland, where he could obtain a cargo of fish in order to help pay the expenses of the voyage. He sailed into the English port of Plymouth in June 1618.

Executed for treason

By then news of the attack on San Tomás had reached James I. The Spanish ambassador was insistent in his demand that Raleigh be punished, and this time the explorer's luck had run out. After failing in an attempt to escape to France, Raleigh was tried and convicted on the treason charges brought against him years earlier. His execution took place on October 29, 1618. As the ill-fated adventurer was about to be beheaded, the executioner asked him to turn his head another way. Raleigh's last words were, "What matter how the head lie, so the heart be right?"

Johannes Rebmann

Born January 16, 1820,
Gerlingen, Germany

Died October 4, 1876,
Kornthal, Germany

Johannes Rebmann was a German missionary who explored the interior of East Africa; he was the first European to see Mount Kilimanjaro.

Johannes Rebmann, like a number of other famous explorers, arrived at his avocation through missionary work. Among other well-known missionary-explorers were **David Livingstone,** who made important discoveries in the lake system of central Africa, and **Johann Ludwig Krapf** (see separate entries), who paved the way for explorers of the Nile River. Rebmann, who worked in East Africa with Krapf, was the first European to see Mount Kilimanjaro, the highest mountain in Africa. At first geographers in Europe did not believe his report because, they said, a snow-capped mountain could not exist at the equator. Rebmann later became widely recognized for his knowledge of African geography.

Rebmann decided at an early age that he wanted to be a missionary. As a young man of 26, he went to Mombasa, a port on the east coast of Africa in what is today Kenya, where he began working with Krapf. Rebmann helped Krapf establish a mission station at Rabai, about 15 miles inland from Mombasa.

Travels to African interior

In October 1847 Rebmann journeyed into the interior to evaluate the prospects for doing missionary work among the nearby peoples and to look for sites for mission stations. The trip took him to the country of the Wateita tribe on the edge of the plateau that rises up from Kenya's coastal plain. Rebmann noted that the plateau stretched on for as far as he could see. Although he was intrigued by the area, he put off further exploration until a later time.

Sights Kilimanjaro

In the spring of 1848 Rebmann went to visit the Chagga people, who lived beyond the Wateita in what is now the border region between Kenya and Tanzania. On May 11, as he traveled into the territory of the Chagga, he saw a high mountain that looked like it was covered by a white cloud. When his guide said it was *beredi,* meaning "cold," Rebmann realized the mountain must be capped with snow. It was in fact the snow-covered peak of Mount Kilimanjaro, which, at 5,895 feet, is the highest mountain in Africa. Rebmann was the first European to see it.

For the next several weeks Rebmann stayed in the village of Masaki, a chief of the Chagga tribe. During his visit he climbed 2,000 feet up a nearby mountain, hoping to get a better view of Kilimanjaro, but the peak was covered with clouds. As he made his way back to Mombasa he noted how beautiful and rich the land was in this part of Africa.

Gets closer to mountain

In November 1848 Rebmann began a more ambitious journey. He planned to travel to the land of the Kikuyu people in what is now central Kenya, not far from the capital of Nairobi. For some reason he turned back instead to the Chagga country, reaching Masaki's village in early December. Having learned that Masaki was not a particularly important chief, Rebmann wanted to travel on to meet Mankinga, the king of the Chagga, to suggest building a mission in his country. Masaki saw that it was to his advantage to serve as the intermediary between the Chagga tribe and the Europeans, so he tried to prevent Rebmann from continuing. Mankinga was soon informed of Rebmann's presence in the area, however, and he sent soldiers to force Masaki to release Rebmann. They escorted the missionary out of Masaki's village on January 4, 1849.

On the way to Mankinga's village Rebmann passed along the lower slopes of Kilimanjaro and saw the "majestic snow-clad summit" by moonlight. He said later that the night on the mountain was as cold as it is in Germany in November. He learned that unlike his guide, the Chagga had a word for "snow" and understood its properties. He was also informed that the Swahilis from the coast thought the mountain was capped with silver.

Sends back reports on Kilimanjaro

Mankinga seemed receptive to the idea of establishing a Christian mission station in his country. After a pleasant visit, Rebmann returned to Rabai, passing the impressive mountain again on his way. He sent reports of Kilimanjaro back to Europe, but his news was met with disbelief. Geographers of the time said he must be mistaken: it was impossible that snow could exist on the equator in Africa. In fact, in 1852 an eminent geographer, W. D. Cooley, would write a book on Africa in which he stated that it was not snow Rebmann had seen; it was actually a light-colored, quartz-like rock that existed on equatorial mountains. Ironically, Cooley had never even traveled to Africa. Rebmann knew what he had seen and he stuck to his story; but it was some time before the snow on Kilimanjaro became an established fact.

Has miserable visit with Mankinga

The missionary made his third journey to the Chagga country in April 1849. He hoped to go as far as the land of the Wanyamwezi, but this expedition would end in failure. As he had done before, Rebmann traveled through Masaki's territory to the headquarters of King Mankinga. This time it was

Mankinga who did not want Rebmann to travel any farther, and he kept the missionary in his village for two weeks. Each day Mankinga took away more and more of the trade goods Rebmann had brought along. Rebmann finally broke down in tears at the king's thievery. Seeming to relent, Mankinga said he would repay Rebmann with tusks of ivory. As Rebmann prepared to leave on June 6, however, Mankinga informed him that it would not be possible to give him the ivory after all. By this time, Rebmann had nothing left, so Mankinga gave him one broken old tusk to trade for enough food to get home.

Rebmann's humiliation was not over yet. As he left the village, the inhabitants lined up to spit on him. This was their usual ceremony when someone was departing and they wished to indicate a peaceful relationship with the traveler. For Rebmann the spitting was the final insult. His party had barely enough to eat on their way home; on July 26 the missionary sent a message asking Krapf for "a bottle of wine and some biscuits."

During Rebmann's absence two new missionaries—Jakob Erhardt and Johannes Wagner—had arrived in Rabai. Both men immediately came down with fever; Wagner died in July 1849. Erhardt recovered, however, and would work closely with Rebmann for years to come. Soon he and Rebmann bought a plot of land in Kisulidini, an area farther south along the coast and opposite the island of Zanzibar. Here they built another mission station.

Recognized as an expert

In 1851 Rebmann traveled to Cairo, where he married an Englishwoman, the recent widow of another German missionary. Returning to East Africa in April 1852, they went to live in Kisulidini. Rebmann continued to make trips into the interior. From these journeys and reports he gathered by talking with Africans, Rebmann and Erhardt published a map in 1856 in a book Krapf wrote about their travels. It showed the interior of Africa to be occupied by one gigantic lake. This body of water, which was later proved to be nonexistent, was assumed to be the source of the Nile River.

As a result of Krapf's publication Rebmann became a noted authority on African geography. When British explorers **Richard Burton** and **John Hanning Speke** (see separate entries) arrived in Africa in January 1857 to search for the sources of the Nile, the first stop they made was to consult with the missionary.

Has poor health in last years

Rebmann maintained the mission post at Kisulidini until 1875. By then his wife had died and he was partially blind. He decided to return to Germany, where he saw his native village again after an absence of 31 years. His health was poor, however, and in the cold climate he contracted pneumonia. The illness left him completely blind. Rebmann's colleague Krapf, who was living in the nearby village of Kornthal, took Rebmann in so he could care for him. A nurse who had known Rebmann as a youth was hired and helped him to recover. They were married shortly thereafter, but Rebmann soon suffered a relapse and died in Kornthal on October 4, 1876.

Sally Ride

Born May 26, 1951,
Encino, California

S ally Ride never dreamed she would be the first American woman to fly in space. Her career as an astronaut began in 1977, when she answered a newspaper ad placed by the National Aeronautics and Space Administration (NASA), which was soliciting applications from young scientists to serve as "mission specialists" on future space flights. After a long process of evaluation, Ride was accepted into the space program, which had previously recruited only male military test pilots.

Ride was not the first woman in space, however. A Russian woman, **Valentina Tereshkova** (see entry), had accompanied a team of astronauts as early as 1963; a second Russian, Svetlana Savitskaya, flew one year before Ride in 1982. But when Ride's mission was successfully accomplished, she became one of the most respected women in the world and a symbol of hope and progress for American women. Since her historic flight in 1983, a number of other women have proven themselves on U.S. space shuttle missions.

Sally Ride, a crew member on the space shuttle Challenger, *was the first American woman to fly in space.*

Early years as an athlete and scholar

Sally Kristen Ride was born in Encino, California, on May 26, 1951. Her father, a professor of political science at a local community college, described the atmosphere in their home as one of kind encouragement. Her mother volunteered as a counselor at a women's correctional institution, and her sister became a Presbyterian minister. The only pressure the Rides put on their children was to do their best.

A gifted athlete, Ride spent much of her early childhood playing baseball and football with neighborhood boys. When she turned her attention to tennis at the age of ten, her natural ability and competitive spirit soon earned her a place on the U.S. junior tennis circuit. She was also awarded a partial scholarship to the Westlake School in Los Angeles. Ride found a mentor in one of her favorite teachers, Dr. Elizabeth Mommaerts, whose interest in science inspired Ride to become an excellent student.

During the next few years, Ride was torn between science and tennis, and for a brief period tennis won. Although in 1968 she enrolled at Swarthmore College in Pennsylvania to study physics, she left after only three semesters to try to become a tennis professional. In spite of concerted effort, however, she decided she would never be good enough to become a top-ranked player. Ride put tennis behind her and in 1970 returned to college at Stanford University in California. She took a double major in physics and English literature, specializing in the works of William Shakespeare. She enjoyed Shakespeare so much she considered pursuing this interest in graduate school; instead, she settled on astrophysics, studying such lofty subjects as X-ray astronomy and free-election lasers.

Application to the NASA space program

In 1977 Ride was among the 8,000 people who applied for the job of mission specialist with the NASA space program. Because of her excellent qualifications, she was one of 208 finalists. NASA's decision to accept women was a direct result of a shift in emphasis in the multi-billion-dollar space shuttle program. In an effort to become more cost-effective, NASA began to develop projects for private industry. When carrying out complex experiments for paying customers, the skills of scientists and technicians became just as important as the expertise of the pilots. After Ride underwent psychiatric evaluations, physical tests, and several personal interviews, she was one of five women accepted in the astronaut class of 1978. Among the women were a surgeon, a biochemist, a geologist, a physicist, and an electrical engineer.

Ride underwent an intensive yearlong training program that included parachute jumping, water survival, adaption to gravitational pull and weightlessness, and radio communications and navigation. She enjoyed earning her pilot's license so much that flying became a favorite hobby. All of the recruits flew hundreds of hours in facsimile spacecraft, or "simulators." Ride was assigned to a team that designed a remote mechanical arm to be used in deploying and retrieving space satellites. This arm proved to be invaluable in subsequent shuttle missions. During the second and third flights of the space shuttle *Columbia* (in November 1981 and March 1982), Ride served as the ground-based communications officer who radioed messages back and forth between the shuttle crew. She was valued for her practical approach to problem solving and her ability to work well with a team.

Assignment as a *Challenger* crew member

Ride's opportunity finally came in March 1982, when Commander Robert Crippen announced that she had been chosen as one of the crew members of the space shuttle *Challenger*. Although Crippen insisted she had not been chosen because she was a woman and even though Ride herself downplayed the importance of this issue, feminists celebrated her participation in the flight as a victory for women. Shortly after she was chosen for the program, she married a fellow astronaut.

Following several months of intensive training, the seventh space shuttle flight, with Ride on board, lifted off at 7:00 A.M., June 18, 1983, from Cape Canaveral, Florida. Turning out to cheer her on were several hundred thousand spectators, many wearing T-shirts on which "Ride, Sally Ride" was printed. When *Challenger* achieved Earth orbit, Ride's duties were to deploy two communications satellites, conduct trials of the mechanical arm she had helped design, and perform and monitor about 40 scientific experiments.

Experiments in space

Ride launched *Anik-C,* a Canadian communications satellite, on the first day of the flight. The next day she successfully deployed *Palapa B,* an Indonesian communications satellite that provided telephone signals to one million people in Southeast Asia. The mission specialists carried out several tests designed by NASA researchers to determine the feasibility of performing certain industrial manufacturing processes in zero gravity. The most important test was an unqualified success—the deployment and recapture of a self-contained 3,300-pound space laboratory built in West Germany. The scientists needed to know if the shuttle could retrieve malfunctioning satellites, make onboard repairs, and return them to orbit.

Challenger landed on June 24, 1983, at Edwards Air Force Base in California. In a postflight press conference, an elated Ride said, "the thing I'll remember most about the flight is that it was fun. In fact, I'm sure it was the most fun that I'll ever have in my life." After three weeks of debriefings, Ride took another assignment at NASA—acting as liaison officer between NASA and private companies doing work on the space program. In October 1983 she flew her last mission on the *Challenger.* Nearly three years later, on January 28, 1986, the *Challenger* exploded upon takeoff, killing all crew members, including schoolteacher Christa McAuliffe, the first civilian to fly in the space shuttle. Ride continues to be a spokesperson for U.S. space efforts.

Susie Carson Rijnhart

Born 1868,
Strathroy, Ontario, Canada

Died February 7, 1908,
Canada

T he life of Canadian missionary Susie Carson Rijnhart is remarkable in many ways. She became a physician when it was extremely difficult for a woman to do so, and as a person with a clear sense of purpose, she learned both Chinese and Tibetan in order to carry out her mission. Proving herself to be a survivor, she suffered a harrowing journey that made her the second European woman to enter and return from Tibet.

Susie Carson was born in the small town of Strathroy in Ontario, Canada, where her father was the Methodist minister. Deciding at an early age that she wanted to be a medical missionary, she graduated from the Woman's Medical College in Toronto in 1888. Six years later she met Petrus Rijnhart, a Dutch missionary who had just returned from China. They married and left immediately for China to continue his work together. They were not sponsored by any church but were financed by donations from friends and their own savings.

Susie Carson Rijnhart was a Canadian missionary who traveled through eastern Tibet in an attempt to reach the Tibetan capital of Lhasa.

Works with husband among Buddhists

The Rijnharts planned to go to Kumbum on the China-Tibet frontier, which was an important center of Buddhist learning and worship. From there, they hoped to travel into the interior of Tibet. Their ultimate goal was to reach the Tibetan capital, Lhasa, where Christian missionaries had been barred since the seventeenth century. They landed in Shanghai and traveled up the Yangtze River to Hsi-ning, the capital of the province of Tsinghai. From there, they went to the small town of Lusar, the trading center for the great Buddhist monastery of Kumbum, which housed over 4,000 monks. They stayed there for two years.

While the Rijnharts were at Kumbum the Muslim inhabitants of the neighboring province of Gansu revolted, and there were many casualties. Although the Rijnharts had set up a clinic in their home to treat patients informally, they were surprised to be invited to the Buddhist lamasery to set up a hospital. They worked day and night, impartially treating both Muslims and Buddhists. During this six-month period, they were able to learn Tibetan and study the Buddhist religion. In her conversations with the head lama, Susie came to appreciate and understand this philosophy, which was so different from Christianity.

Couple travels to Tibet

Feeling that their mission in Kumbum had been successful and confident of their ability to speak Tibetan, the Rijnharts moved on to another trading town, Tankar. They were visited by several adventurers who were traveling through central Asia, including Swedish explorer **Sven Hedin** (see entry). The Rijnharts themselves made an exploring expedition with their newborn baby boy, Charlie, to a sacred lake, Koko Nor. On this trip they decided that they wanted to travel to Lhasa and see if they could continue their missionary work. They knew this would be difficult because the city was closed to all foreigners, and no Western woman had ever been there.

The Rijnharts left Tankar with Charlie, their dog Topsy, and three servants on May 20, 1898, and traveled into Tibet.

They celebrated Charlie's first birthday on June 30 with a cake. His mother wrote:

> How thoroughly baby enjoyed those days, when he made the tents ring with joyousness from his musical laughter, his shouts and the beating of our Russian brass wash-basin which he used as a drum. Then from sheer weariness he would fall asleep, leaving the camp pervaded by a stillness, made sweet by the fact that he was still there.

Experience hardship and tragedy

After three months, when the Rijnharts were within 200 miles of Lhasa, their two guides deserted them. Then one of their horses, which they depended on for transport, died; five others were stolen. The worst was yet to come, when on "the darkest day in our history," baby Charlie simply stopped breathing and died without any warning. Susie wrote, "The very joy of our life, the only human thing that made life and labour sweet amid the desolation and isolation of Tibet—the child of our love" was dead. They buried him that night in a medicine box, and "in his hand was placed a little bunch of white asters and blue poppies"; the bereaved parents continued on their way the next day.

At Nagchuka the Rijnharts were told they could not proceed any farther and were turned back. They were, however, given fresh horses and supplies. Along the road, on September 15, 1898, they stopped to have a picnic to celebrate their fourth wedding anniversary. They were ambushed by a gang of robbers, who stole as many horses as they could travel with and shot most of the others. To prevent pursuit, they crippled one horse by shooting it in the spine. They even took the Rijnharts' dog, Topsy. After the attack, the porters said they would go to get help, but they disappeared. The Rijnharts were left with one old gray pony and a few of their supplies.

Susie left alone

By this time they were assailed by winter blizzards.

Unable to carry a heavy load, they gathered a minimum of provisions and set off. On the third day, they reached a wide river and saw an encampment on the other side. That night they pitched camp in a snowstorm. The next morning, Petrus crossed the river and headed to the encampment to get help. He disappeared behind a rock and was never seen again.

Susie was abandoned. After waiting for several days, she went on. She quickly learned about the status of women in Tibet: she was given almost no assistance and was not allowed to enter a tent. She spent several nights sleeping outside in the snow with the dogs. Her possessions were stolen or she had to use them to pay for guides. She even had to sell her Bible and her baby's fur coat and boots in order to eat. Finally, two months after her husband disappeared, Rijnhart arrived, starving and with frostbitten feet, at the Christian mission station of Ta-chien-lu in western China. She announced, "I am Dr. Rijnhart."

Returns to Canada

Rijnhart stayed at the mission station for six months to recuperate. She eventually found out that her husband had been killed by robbers, probably the same ones who had attacked them on the road. When she was well, she returned to Canada, where she wrote about her experiences and lectured to Christian audiences. Feeling that her work was not completed, she returned to Ta-chien-lu in 1902. In 1905 she married a fellow missionary, a Mr. Moyes. She became ill in 1907 and went back to Canada; she died on February 7, 1908, leaving her husband with a three-week-old son.

Jacob Roggeveen

Born 1659,
Holland

Died 1729,
Holland

One of the great legends that circulated among countries pursuing the exploration of the world was the possible existence of a vast southern continent. This land was imagined to encompass Antarctica's South Pole and extend far into the South Seas, or the Pacific Ocean. The discovery of Australia, as well as much of the islands of the South Pacific, was the result of the search for this continent. Various expeditions whittled away at its contours by degrees over a period of many years. Finally explorers realized that Antarctica was not connected to Australia or to any other great landmass.

Pursues father's dream

Jacob Roggeveen was a Dutchman who, late in life, decided to undertake a voyage his father had dreamed of making to search for Terras Australis, the great southern continent. Roggeveen's father had interested the Dutch West India Company in the search for the continent, but he died before he was

Jacob Roggeveen was a Dutch navigator who made a trip to the Pacific Ocean to find the great southern continent; he was the first European to visit Easter Island.

able to make the expedition. Roggeveen worked for a competing company, the Dutch East India Company, from which he eventually retired with a large fortune.

In 1721, at the age of 62, he decided to pursue his father's dream of going to the South Pacific. The Dutch West India Company agreed to participate by outfitting three ships for the expedition, which left Holland in August 1721. The ships sailed down through the South Atlantic to the Falkland Islands and then rounded Cape Horn at the southern tip of South America. In doing so they passed into the Pacific Ocean. Roggeveen sailed north to the Juan Fernandez Islands, which lie off the coast of Chile. He noted that these small islands would serve as the ideal base for a Dutch colony from which to search for the southern continent.

Discovers Easter Island

Roggeveen sailed west, fully expecting that he would soon sight the edge of the continent. Instead, on Easter Sunday of 1722, he came upon a small island, which he named in honor of the day. Easter Island is the easternmost of the Polynesian islands. Because of its isolation, the Polynesian inhabitants had developed a unique culture. The most remarkable cultural feature of these people was the huge statues of heads they had carved from stone, called Moais. Apparently they worshiped these statues as gods. The Dutchmen with Roggeveen were the first Europeans to see the carvings.

Some of the Polynesians were killed in initial contacts with the Dutch. Roggeveen considered the islanders to be friendly, however, although they tended to take the Europeans' possessions without asking. Roggeveen left the island after only a week, convinced that he would shortly reach the southern continent.

Visits other islands

Roggeveen sailed generally northwestward but often changed his course, always thinking the continent was just over the horizon. The three ships sailed 800 leagues (about

2,400 miles), but the Dutchmen did not see any land. Finally they came upon the northern islands in the Tuamotu Archipelago, which are now part of French Polynesia, where they encountered trouble. After one of the ships was wrecked on a coral reef they had a confrontation with the inhabitants of the island of Makatéa; some of the islanders were shot and ten Dutchmen were stoned to death.

Roggeveen and his men decided that since they had not yet found the southern continent, they should sail directly to Batavia, the capital of the Dutch East Indies. From there they planned to take the usual route back to Holland. On their way westward, they passed the island of Bora, which is part of the Society Islands, and the Samoan Islands, where they went ashore to get fresh water and fruit. The Dutch ships passed between the island groups of Tuvalu and Kiribati and headed north of New Guinea to the Moluccas (Spice Islands), which were part of the Dutch East Indies. From there, they went to

These seven Moais, heads of gods carved from stone, date from the thirteenth century. Roggeveen and his crew were the first Europeans to see these carvings on Easter Island.

Java and the great port of Batavia, which is today called Djakarta. They anchored in Batavia in September 1722.

Sent back to Holland

Roggeveen's party did not receive a warm welcome in Batavia. The governor and other officials all worked for the East India Company, which had a monopoly on Dutch trade east of Holland. Since Roggeveen was associated with the West India Company, he was considered a trespasser. His ships were confiscated, and he and his men were sent back to Holland almost as prisoners on ships of the East India Company. When he reached his home country, Roggeveen started legal proceedings to get back the value of his ships and eventually succeeded.

Adds to knowledge of Pacific

The Dutch navigator had not found the great southern continent. He had, however, traveled extensively throughout the waters of the South Pacific, adding to geographic knowledge of the day. His trip did not resolve the question of the continent's existence, but it helped other navigators to know which areas still remained to be explored. Perhaps most important, Roggeveen had discovered Easter Island, which would become a site of great interest to anthropologists.

However, there were no other visitors from the West for another 50 years. By that time, the population of the island was much smaller because of continuous warfare between rival clans. The Easter Islanders who were left had lost the knowledge of how the stone carvings were made. It is unfortunate that Roggeveen did not take more time to find out about this culture and its achievements, which are now considered so remarkable and mysterious.

Friedrich Gerhard Rohlfs

Born April 14, 1831,
Near Bremen, Germany

Died June 2, 1896,
Germany

G erhard Rohlfs was an adventurer whose aimless wanderings contributed greatly to knowledge of the maps of Africa. Although he was the first European to cross West Africa from the Mediterranean to the Gulf of Guinea, his place in history is based on his extensive chronicles of his journeys over a 20-year period. His accounts, which were widely read, helped to shape German public opinion about Africa and Africans; today they give us a valuable insight into the way Victorians looked at exploration.

Gerhard Rohlfs was born near Bremen in Germany in 1831. The third son of a doctor, he was educated at home until he was 15; once he got to school he hated it. He ran away to Amsterdam, but his parents caught up with him and brought him back home. At the age of 18 he quit school and joined the army in order to fight in the war between the German Confederation and Denmark over the region of Schleswig-Holstein. At the end of the war, he spent some time at various universi-

> *Gerhard Rohlfs was a German adventurer who was the first European to cross West Africa from the Mediterranean Sea to the Gulf of Guinea.*

ties as a medical student. Giving up the study of medicine, he enlisted in the Austrian army, from which he deserted.

Seeks adventure in Africa

In North Africa Rohlfs joined the French Foreign Legion, which was known for attracting loners, adventurers, and men who wanted to escape their pasts. Rohlfs arrived in Algeria in 1855 and fought in the Kabylia campaigns of 1856 and 1857. Because of his medical background, he was promoted to sergeant and acting surgeon. He stayed in the Foreign Legion until 1861, when he headed for Morocco to try to obtain a job as a doctor in the army of the sultan of Morocco.

Setting out from Tangier on the Mediterranean coast, he disguised himself as a Muslim because he thought it would be easier to travel that way. No one was ever completely fooled by the disguise and his supposed Muslim religious conversion, but it probably saved his life a few times. After being robbed of all his money he safely reached Ouezzane, where he was given a letter of recommendation by the grand sherif. From there he went to Meknes and became a physician in the court of the sultan.

Injured in robbery

Rohlfs stayed in the sultan's court for a while but became interested in seeing other parts of Africa. In 1862 he left in order to travel to the south. He went as far south as Tafilalt, an oasis in the southern Atlas Mountains. He was the first European to visit the city since French explorer **René Caillié** (see entry) in 1828. In the oasis of Bou-Am, north of Tafilalt, Rohlfs was attacked by robbers and left for dead. He had been shot through the thigh, and his left arm and right hand were almost cut off. Two passersby found him and took him to the oasis of Hadjui, where he recuperated for two months. Left with a shortened arm and no feeling in the fingers of his right hand, he was bothered by pain for the rest of his life. He then headed across the border to the French outpost of Géryville in Algeria.

Gains fame as explorer

Rohlfs traveled to Oran and Algiers in order to try to regain his health. In 1864 he made a visit to the region of Tuat in southern Algeria, becoming the first European to travel there. He did not make it to Timbuktu, which had been his objective. This was his most significant expedition because it yielded new information about Saharan oases and trade routes. By this time he had sent some of his reports to a German geographical magazine, and he was beginning to become well known as an African explorer. On a visit to Germany in 1865 he was persuaded by **Heinrich Barth** (see entry) to try to discover the relationship between the rivers flowing into Lake Chad and the Niger-Benue system.

Rohlfs left Tripoli in May 1865, crossing the Sahara by way of Marzuq to Kukawa, then going on to Bornu. He reached the Benue River at Lokoja on March 28, 1867; he sailed down the Benue to the Niger and on to the Gulf of Guinea near Lagos. In making this trip, he became the first European to cross western Africa from the Mediterranean to the Gulf of Guinea. On his return to Germany he was given many honors and met personally with the Prussian king and Chancellor Otto von Bismarck.

Sought out by other explorers

Rohlfs was sent as an official observer on Sir Robert Napier's military expedition to Ethiopia in 1868. He went back to Tripoli at the end of 1868 and was entrusted with some gifts from the king of Prussia to the king of Bornu. He turned them over to Gustav Nachtigal, who was instrumental in founding the German empire in Africa, and sent him off into the Sahara.

During this period Rohlfs was married to an 18-year-old niece of a fellow German explorer. They established a home in the artistic center of Weimar. Now considered an authority on African exploration, Rohlfs entertained a wide circle of respectful friends and admirers. He lectured frequently, and was consulted by other explorers eager for advice.

Takes last trip to Africa

In the following years Rohlfs went as far east as the Nile, then explored the fringes of the highlands of Ethiopia. In 1876 he attended a conference sponsored by King Leopold of Belgium on African exploration in Brussels. After the conference he participated in a disastrous expedition that traveled from Benghazi to Aujila and across the desert to the oases at Al-Kufrah. From the beginning there were rumors that the caravan would be ambushed by robbers. Covering over 50 miles a day for five days, the party had become prisoners of their hostile guides by the time they reached their destination. The camp was ransacked and supplies and money were stolen. Through the intervention of a friendly tribe, the party escaped with their lives. This proved to be Rohlfs's last expedition to Africa.

Goes into semi-retirement

Rohlfs was sent on a diplomatic mission to the court of the emperor of Ethiopia in 1879. Five years later he was named German consul in Zanzibar but got into conflict with the British consul and was quickly recalled. He then refused offers of consulates in other places and went back to a life of semi-retirement in Germany, writing about his adventures in a series of popular books that earned him a great deal of money. He led a prosperous and leisurely life until his death from a heart condition in June 1896.

Despite his ability to get along with others and his great popularity, Rohlfs has been called the "lonely" explorer. His small, modest caravans contrasted vividly with the huge entourages that accompanied many African explorers. Rohlfs was most successful when he traveled alone with a minimum of equipment and advisers, and with only the most obscure of objectives. It is thought that his fascination with the vast, empty stretches of the African continent and his willingness to cast himself adrift in search of the unknown must have fulfilled a longing deep within his soul.

Dick Rutan

Born 1939,
Loma Linda, California

Jeana Yeager

Born 1952,
Fort Worth, Texas

Jeana Yeager and Dick Rutan ▶

A fortunate coincidence brought Jeana Yeager and Dick Rutan to the same air show in California in 1980. They met, became friends, and soon began to work together. Eventually they shared a dream of piloting a plane around the world without stopping or refueling. In realizing that dream, they made history. Credit must also go to another member of the team, Dick's brother Burt, who had a reputation as the most innovative airplane designer of his time.

Dick Rutan and Jeana Yeager are American pilots who flew an experimental airplane around the world without stopping or refueling.

Rutan has early interest in aviation

Dick Rutan was born in Loma Linda, California, near Los Angeles in 1939. Following World War II his father, a dentist, moved the family to the small town of Dinuba near Fresno, where Dick and his brother Burt became obsessed with flying and airplanes. Rutan started taking flying lessons at the age of 15; he made his first solo flight and got his pilot's license on his sixteenth birthday, the earliest legal age. When

Dick Rutan
Jeana Yeager

he graduated from high school he enlisted in the U.S. Air Force and trained to become a navigator.

After serving in Vietnam Rutan was accepted for fighter pilot training; he returned to Vietnam in 1967. On his last combat mission he had to eject from a burning airplane. He was then assigned to Europe but resigned from the air force when he failed to receive a promotion he had sought. After he left the air force he separated from his wife and went to work as a test pilot for Burt's company, which manufactured and sold experimental airplanes.

Yeager flies for Rutan company

Jeana Yeager grew up in Texas, where her father was an engineer for a defense contractor. Her love of horses, which began when she was a very young girl, became a lifelong interest and, briefly, her profession. In 1972 Yeager married a deputy sheriff and moved to Rosenberg, Texas, near Houston. After five years of marriage she left her husband and moved to California, where she took a job drafting and surveying for a geothermal energy company in Santa Rosa. Pursuing her avid interest in flying, she received her pilot's license in 1978. When she met Rutan at the air show in Chino, California, the Rutan company was demonstrating its experimental aircraft.

Yeager went to work with the Rutan Aircraft Factory and broke several speed records with the specially designed Rutan planes. Over lunch one day in 1981, the two Rutan brothers and Yeager came up with the idea of trying to break existing records by designing a plane that would fly around the world with no stops or refueling. It took five years of tremendous effort to build the plane that Burt Rutan designed.

Fund-raising is difficult

Spending most of their time trying to raise money to finance the plane, which they had named the *Voyager,* Rutan and Yeager each lived a subsistence-level life. Initially they were frustrated in their efforts to interest large corporations in an opportunity to make aviation history because companies were reluctant to invest in risky ventures. Determined to make their project an all-American effort, Rutan and Yeager even turned down an offer of financial backing from another country. To raise money they sold T-shirts, spoke to service clubs, recruited volunteers, and formed the "Voyager Important People Club." Just when they thought their prospects were hopeless, a financial contributor who had faith in the project kept it going a while longer.

Voyager has special design

Burt Rutan's challenge was to build a very light airplane large enough to carry enough fuel for a round-the-world flight. His design was based on an H-shape with the main wing toward the rear and the stabilizing wing in front. The wingspan was 111 feet, longer than that of a 727 jetliner. There was little metal in the plane, since the body was made of a composite material consisting mainly of epoxy. The plane had two engines: the 110-horsepower engine in the rear could produce a cruising speed of 80 miles per hour, and the more powerful engine in front was used for takeoffs and landings.

Test flight sets record

In July 1986 Rutan and Yeager took the *Voyager* on a nonstop, four-and-a-half-day test flight up and down the California coast. During the flight one of the two pilots would sit at the controls while the other would stretch out and rest in the narrow, three-foot-wide space. It was difficult to eat and drink in such close quarters. Yeager, who consumed less than a gallon of water during the flight, fainted during the postflight press conference. She and Rutan had set a world record for distance and endurance.

The pilots continued their test flights in preparation for the round-the-world trip, scheduled for mid-September 1986. After one test, however, the trip was postponed because part of the plane's front propeller had broken off. Rutan and Yeager decided to reschedule the flight for December in spite of the fact that they would be flying around the Northern Hemisphere in winter.

Dick Rutan
Jeana Yeager

Winds and storms affect flight

Rutan and Yeager left Edwards Air Force Base in California on December 14, 1986. Since this was the first time the *Voyager* had been flown with a full load of fuel, the weight caused the tips of the wings to dip and to scrape off the winglets at right angles to the wings. Rutan, who piloted the plane throughout most of the trip, was able to shake off the damaged material and continue the flight.

They flew into the Pacific and, near the Philippines, ran into Typhoon Marge, which was producing 80 mile-per-hour winds. Yet this danger proved to be an advantage: the typhoon's tail winds pushed the *Voyager* along so that it reached the fastest speed of the trip, 147 miles per hour. Rutan and Yeager slept for two or three hours at a time; they ate pre-cooked meals and took food supplements.

When they were over Malaysia on their way across the Indian Ocean and Africa, they ran into storms that forced them

Dick Rutan
Jeana Yeager

to fly at higher and less fuel-efficient altitudes than they had planned. Sometimes they had to use both engines in order to avoid turbulence. Yeager was badly bruised when the plane was tossed around by strong winds. The two pilots suffered mood swings that alternated from euphoria to despair, depending on the weather and the flight's progress.

Pilots set record

Off the west coast of Africa, they ran into an unexpected storm, and Rutan lost control of the plane for a short time. A little farther along, the oil warning light came on: one engine almost overheated because the pilots were so tired they forgot to check the oil level. They flew over Central America in the dark with Yeager at the controls. In spite of all their difficulties, they landed at Edwards Air Force Base on December 23, 1986, a day ahead of schedule, with Yeager cranking down the landing gear by hand. When the *Voyager* touched down on the runway it had only about 10 of its original 1,200 gallons of fuel. The nine-day flight had covered 25,012 miles, more than twice the distance of the previous record for an un-refueled flight.

Pilots and plane receive national recognition

Rutan and Yeager were received by enthusiastic crowds as they traveled around the United States. They were presented with a medal by President Ronald Reagan. Corporate sponsorships and a royalty advance on a book about the flight enabled them to pay off the debt they still owed from constructing the plane. The *Voyager* was placed in the National Air and Space Museum at the Smithsonian Institution in Washington, D.C. This was an especially meaningful moment for Rutan and Yeager because it was in this museum that they had promised themselves the *Voyager* would be an American technological breakthrough. They had accomplished their feat in the best tradition of Orville and Wilbur Wright, Charles Lindbergh, and other heroes of American aviation.

Dick Rutan
Jeana Yeager

Ernest Shackleton

*Born February 17, 1874,
Kilkea, Kildare, Ireland*

*Died January 5, 1922,
South Georgia Island, Antarctica*

Sir Ernest Shackleton, a British explorer, made four voyages to Antarctica. During his second voyage he came within 97 nautical miles (112 statute miles) of the South Pole.

Ernest Henry Shackleton, the son of a doctor, was born in Ireland on February 17, 1874. When he was ten years old, his family moved to London, where he was educated at Dulwich College, later part of the University of London. Determined to become a sailor, Shackleton left school at age 16 and joined the merchant marine.

In 1901 he was appointed third lieutenant on the *Discover-er,* the ship that the British explorer Robert Scott was outfitting for the first scientific expedition of Antarctica. During the expedition Shackleton was chosen to accompany Scott and the zoologist Dr. Edward Wilson on a journey by sledge across the Ross Ice Shelf to the southernmost point yet reached in Antarctica (82°17' S). On the return journey all three men suffered a severe case of scurvy, a disease caused by a lack of vitamin C. Shackleton became especially ill. He was sent back to Britain on a supply ship, but he vowed to return to continue his explorations in Antarctica.

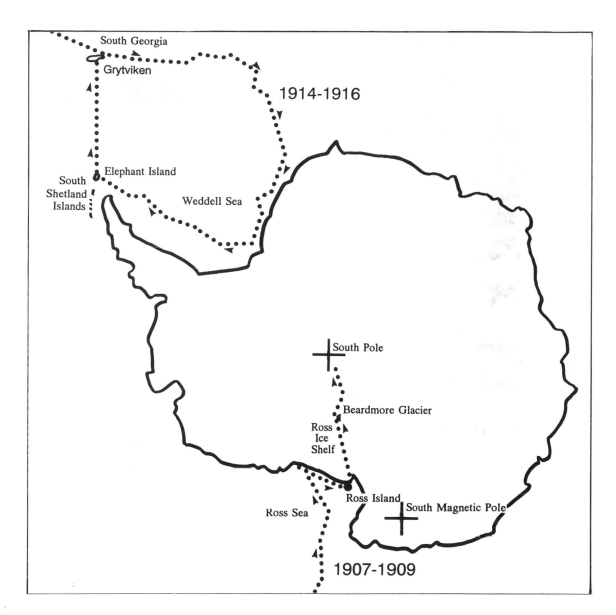

South Georgia

Grytviken

1914-1916

Elephant Island

South
Shetland
Islands

Weddell Sea

South Pole

Beardmore Glacier

Ross
Ice
Shelf

Ross Island

South Magnetic Pole

Ross Sea

1907-1909

Leader of an Antarctic expedition

After Shackleton had recovered, he went to work briefly as a journalist. He was then appointed to the post of secretary of the Scottish Geographical Society in Edinburgh, Scotland. In 1906 he took time out to run for a seat in Parliament. Although Shackleton lost the election, he took advantage of his position at the Scottish Geographical Society by lobbying

On his 1907-09 expedition Shackleton came within only 97 nautical miles of the South Pole. During an exploring trip in 1914-16, he and his crew were stranded for nine months in the Weddell Sea.

wealthy patrons to support his own expedition to Antarctica. By 1907 he had received enough private contributions to finance a trip to both the South Pole and the South Magnetic Pole.

Shackleton planned to reach Antarctica by using dogs, ponies, and an automobile that had been modified to pull sledges. He also intended to record the entire expedition with a movie camera. The Shackleton expedition, which included the Australian explorer and geologist Douglas Mawson, sailed from England on the *Nimrod* on August 7, 1907.

Journey across the Ross Ice Shelf

After a brief stop in New Zealand, the party proceeded to Antarctica. Before Shackleton left England, he had received a letter from Scott saying Scott intended to make another assault on the South Pole and asking Shackleton not to use the previous Scott expedition base on Ross Island at McMurdo Sound. At the time, Shackleton had agreed to Scott's request, but when he reached the edge of the Ross Ice Shelf, he found the only place his ship could land was at the western end of Ross Island, near Scott's old base.

Shackleton, whose men had nicknamed him "The Boss," set up his hut at Cape Royds on Ross Island in February 1908. The following month three members of the expedition climbed Mount Erebus, an active volcano on Ross Island. At the end of the Antarctic winter in September, Shackleton and his men began setting up supply depots on the Ross Island Shelf. Using ponies for transportation, the main team, consisting of Shackleton and three companions, started out from Cape Royds at the end of October. In early November they broke Scott's previous record for the southernmost point reached in Antarctica. After a brief celebration they continued on their journey.

Hardships on the voyage

In early December, when they came to the end of the ice shelf, they discovered a glacier, which Shackleton named Beardmore Glacier in honor of his principal financial backer.

The party then climbed the glacier, crossing to the central plateau of Antarctica on Christmas Day. In spite of their success, Shackleton's party faced many hazards. By the time they had reached the plateau, all of their ponies had died, and the men, who had run short of rations, were forced to eat the carcasses.

In early January 1909 they had come within only 97 nautical miles of the South Pole. Realizing they could go no farther, however, Shackleton ordered his men to turn back. The party's fortunes worsened on the return trip. Having difficulty spotting their supply depots, they nearly starved to death.

In the meantime, another member of Shackleton's expedition, Edgeworth David, and a small group of explorers had arrived at the South Magnetic Pole on January 16, 1901. When David's party returned to the base at Cape Royds on February 26, they met the *Nimrod*. Fearing the approach of winter, the *Nimrod* crew left the base without Shackleton and his men, who had failed to appear. When Shackleton's party arrived on February 28, they found themselves abandoned. They signaled wildly, and the next morning the *Nimrod* picked them up.

Knighthood and fame

When he reached England in June 1909, Shackleton discovered he had become a popular hero. In addition to being knighted by King Edward VII, he received £20,000 from the British government for paying off his debts, and he was awarded a gold medal by the Royal Geographical Society. Shackleton wrote a book about his attempt to reach the South Pole, *The Heart of the Antarctic,* which was published in 1909. Within the next few years the South Pole was reached by the Norwegian explorer **Roald Amundsen** (see entry) and by Scott, who did not return alive. Craving adventure, Shackleton conceived an ambitious plan—to travel all the way across Antarctica from the Weddell Sea to the Ross Sea.

Because of Shackleton's formidable fund-raising skills, he was able to raise enough money to equip two ships, although he needed only one, which he named the *Endurance*.

His party was prepared to sail on August 1, 1914, when World War I broke out. To help the war effort, Shackleton offered the *Endurance* to the British government, but Winston Churchill, first lord of the admiralty, turned down his generous offer. Churchill told Shackleton to proceed with his expedition, so the *Endurance* left port a week later.

Perilous return to Antarctica

On December 7 Shackleton and his party reached the Weddell Sea, threading their way in the *Endurance* through the ice until they came close to the Antarctica mainland at a stretch of coast known as Coats Land. Heading for safe anchorage, the ship became trapped in the ice. Shackleton stayed on board throughout the long Antarctic winter. The sun set on May 1 and did not reappear until July 26, by which time the ice had begun to break up. It was impossible to free the *Endurance*, however, and it became battered by the pressure of the cracking ice. In late October the ship began to leak badly, so Shackleton and his crew unloaded their supplies; they set up camp on a large ice floe one and a half miles from the disabled ship, which sank about a month later.

Shackleton's plan was to walk across the ice field to Paulet Island, 350 miles away, where he knew there was a supply depot. They set out on December 20, dragging their boats with them. On January 1, 1916, they were set adrift on a large ice floe, which carried them north, and by March 17 they were 60 miles from Paulet Island. Ice conditions were so severe, however, that they could not reach the island. Shackleton set his sights instead on reaching Elephant Island at the tip of the Palmer Peninsula. The party abandoned the ice floe and boarded their boats on April 9. As they were resting on a floe one night, it split in two, and Shackleton had to pull one man out of the water by grabbing his sleeping bag. They reached Elephant Island on April 15, 1916.

Several days later, after realizing they could not live long on the desolate, ice-covered island, Shackleton took five companions and headed out in a boat to seek help. On the second day they were hit by a blizzard, and on the tenth day a gigantic wave nearly sank them. On the sixteenth day they reached South Georgia Island, nearly wrecking on the shore when a sudden storm swept over them. Once ashore on May 15, Shackleton set out with two men to travel across the island to the small whaling station of Grytviken on the north shore; the rest of the men were too sick to move. Shackleton and his companions walked for 24 hours straight to Grytviken, the first time anyone had crossed the island.

After they had rested and eaten, one of Shackleton's party led a team to rescue the crew members on the other side of the island. Shackleton and the other man headed out in a whaling ship to find the remaining crew on Elephant Island. The ship was not able to make its way through the pack ice. The Uruguayan government sent a ship to retrieve them, but it was also forced back. Shackleton then chartered a British ship, but its engine broke down along the way. It was not until August 20, 1916, that the Chilean steamer *Yelcho* reached the stranded men on Elephant Island. Miraculously, they were still alive.

Final expedition

Upon his return to England, Shackleton served in the expeditionary force that went to northern Russia in 1919. He also wrote *South,* a book about his boat trip to South Georgia Island, which has been called one of the most dramatic stories of exploration ever written. At the end of World War I, he was determined to achieve his goal of crossing Antarctica.

He set out again in September 1921 accompanied by many of his former colleagues, including **Hubert Wilkins** (see entry), who would later attempt to fly across Antarctica. During the voyage Shackleton became ill, so the ship anchored in Grytviken Harbor on South Georgia Island. In the early morning hours of January 5, 1922, Shackleton died of a massive heart attack. He was buried on a hill above the whaling station, where his grave still stands. The remaining members of the expedition tried to continue sailing toward Antarctica, but they were caught in the ice. In April they were forced to return to England.

Nain Singh

Born c. 1832,
India

Died c. 1882,
India

Indian explorer Nain Singh, the first of the British-trained "pundits," made three trips into Tibet.

Upon presenting Nain Singh a gold medal on behalf of the Royal Geographical Society of Great Britain in 1878, the viceroy of India, Colonel Henry Yule, remarked that Singh's "observations have added a larger amount of important knowledge to the map of Asia than those of any living man." Singh not only had a brilliant career as a mapmaker but also repeatedly risked his life as a spy for Great Britain. He was the first of the Indian "pundits" who were trained by the British to go where Westerners were forbidden entry.

British interests in Asia

During the 1800s the major world powers were determined to open up previously unexplored areas for trade and access to resources. Russia and China had competing interests in the Far East. Under the rule of Queen Victoria, Great Britain had acquired an empire that stretched around the world. India was considered its most important colony.

In 1852 Thomas George Montgomerie, a British army engineer, joined the Great Trigonometrical Survey with the mission of mapping all of India. By 1864 he had completed mapping the domains of the maharajah of Jammu and Kashmir, located in northwestern India, which was a considerable accomplishment. At that point, however, Montgomerie encountered a problem. Many parts of India were off-limits to Westerners.

India is bordered on the north by the snowcapped and sometimes impassable Himalaya Mountains, a formidable natural barrier that has served to isolate small neighboring states, such as Nepal, Sikkim, and Bhutan. Tibet was even more remote and tempting to British ambitions. Suspicious of British power, these states absolutely prohibited English explorers from entering their territory.

Establishment of the pundit school

Wanting to know what was on the other side of the mountains, Montgomerie had an inspiration. He sent Abdul Hamid, a Muslim clerk in his office, to Yarkand, a tiny province in what was then Chinese Turkistan, one of the places where Europeans were denied entry. Staying there for six months, Hamid accurately calculated the location of Yarkand and was able to spy on Russian activities in the area. Although Hamid died on his trip back to India, his notes were delivered to Montgomerie. Elated by Hamid's success, Montgomerie proposed that a school be set up to train Indians to penetrate Tibet and bring back information to the British in India. The Indian recruits were called "pundits," an English word of Hindu origin meaning learned man or teacher.

In looking for Indians who might make good pundits, Montgomerie turned to a family who had previously worked for both English and German explorers. Nain Singh was the headmaster of a village school when he and his cousin Mani Singh were selected by Montgomerie for the training program. In two years they had learned to use surveying instruments, navigational astronomy, and altitude calculation methods.

Other famous pundits

Unlike the other pundits, Kintup (born 1849) was a completely untrained and illiterate native of Sikkim, a kingdom bordering India in the Himalayas. Given the code name "K.P.," he was teamed in 1880 with a Mongolian lama, or spiritual leader, and pretended to be his servant; their assignment was to travel to the Tsangpo River in Tibet and find out if it was the same as the Brahmaputra River, which flows through Assam in India. Six years later, after a series of adventures and some difficulty in persuading people to believe his story, Kintup was able to prove he had explored more of the Tsangpo than any previous explorer. He also established the river's connection to the Brahmaputra.

Another pundit, Hari Ram, traveled under the code names "M.H." and "No. 9." He made four expeditions (1871-85) to the area of Mount Everest, the highest mountain in the Himalayas. He surveyed 844 miles that were completely unknown to Western geographers, and he added 420 miles to the survey of the Indian government. Among his major achievements were making the first recorded trip around Mount Everest and tracing the course of the Dudh Kosi River at the base of Mount Everest.

Known by his code name "Krishna" or his code initials "A.K.," Kishen Singh (1850-1921) was a cousin of Nain Singh. He was the youngest pundit when he was put in charge of four assistants in 1872 and sent to Koko Nor near the Chinese border with Tibet. During his second expedition in 1878, he earned his reputation as one of the greatest pundits; while waiting over a year for a Mongolian caravan that would take him to Koko Nor, he mapped the city and environs of Lhasa, the capital of Tibet. His final trip into Tibet lasted four and a half years and covered 2,800 miles; at one point he was forced to ride a horse for 230 miles through bandit country, and he calculated the distance by comparing the horse's stride with his own. Years later his calculations were found to be off by only one mile.

The pundits were also trained to be spies. They would travel with luggage that had secret compartments and would wear clothes with hidden pockets. They would also carry Tibetan prayer wheels containing blank paper on which coded notes could be written. One of the pundits' achievements was perfecting their walk so that each pace was exactly the same length, thus allowing them to accurately measure distances. They were able to keep count of how many paces they walked by using Buddhist prayer beads that had been shortened from the usual length of 108 beads to 100. The pundits were given code names to conceal their true identities. Nain Singh was known simply as "the pundit" or the "chief pundit."

First mission to Tibet

Nain Sigh and his cousin Mani Singh began their first mission to Tibet in January 1865, reaching Katmandu, Nepal, two months later. They were turned back at the Tibetan border town of Kyirong by a suspicious governor, who did not believe their story about why they wanted to enter Tibet. The cousins separated, and Nain Singh joined a caravan posing as a merchant. This time he crossed the border successfully. Singh eventually entered Jih-k'a-tse, the second-largest city in Tibet. It was in Jih-k'a-tse that he was summoned to meet the country's second-highest religious authority, the Panchen Lama, who turned out to be only 11 years old.

Singh arrived in Lhasa, the capital of Tibet, in January 1866, one year after he had left the training camp. It was then that his real work began. By making a total of 20 solar and stellar observations, he came close to calculating the exact latitude of Lhasa for the first time in history. He made 16 thermometer readings every day for almost two weeks. Using the boiling point of water, he calculated Lhasa's altitude at 11,700 feet above sea level, which is near the figure generally accepted today.

Although Singh was invited to the great palace of Potala for a group audience with the twelfth Dalai Lama—who was two years older than the Panchen Lama—he found the other Tibetans were becoming suspicious of his identity. Fearing he would be executed if he were captured, Singh rejoined his caravan and traveled along the main east-west trade route of Tibet. His major triumph on this part of the trip was charting the Tsangpo River from its source to its junction with the Kyi-Chu River. After then being attacked and held captive, Singh finally found his way back to India in July 1867; Mani Singh also returned at that time. The journey had lasted over two years. Singh had by that time walked 1,200 miles and had counted 2,500,000 steps. Montgomerie wrote a letter to the Royal Geographical Society about Singh's outstanding performance.

Search for gold

Singh brought back reports of seeing large golden Buddhas in Tibet. The British had always believed that Tibet held vast quantities of gold; therefore, Singh's second mission, in May 1867, was to investigate the goldfields at Thok Jalung in western Tibet and to plot the location of Ka-erh, Tibet's largest western city. He was accompanied by his brother, Kalian Singh, who had been trained as a pundit; Mani Singh also joined them. At the Mana Pass on the border of Tibet, the three pundits encountered severe blizzards that delayed them until July. Once they had crossed the Tibetan frontier, they were met by Tibetan nomads, who guessed that Singh and his companions were spies. The pundits bribed the leader of the nomads and left Mani Singh as a hostage; however, the two brothers never thought of turning back.

According to a previous plan, Kalian Singh set off on a separate route. Nain traveled alone to the goldfields, which were located on a bleak and desolate plain at 16,000 feet, possibly the highest inhabited place in the world. The gold mine was a mile-long trench about 25 feet deep. The chief of the goldfield, who met Singh in his tent while sipping tea and smoking his water pipe, was immediately suspicious of the pundit. He looked curiously at Singh's well-constructed wood box with secret compartments that concealed surveying instruments, thinking it was too elegant for a simple Indian traveler. Singh was able to bribe the man with some coral jewelry for his wife. Singh stayed five days, reporting back to the British that the mine held considerable wealth. He even saw one nugget that weighed two pounds.

In the meantime, Kalian Singh was exploring the Sutlej River, one of the "Five Rivers" of the Punjab in southwestern Tibet. He reached a tributary called the Gartang, which proved to be the main source of the Indus River. He also managed to free Mani Singh from the nomads and then rejoined his brother. On their way back to India, Nain Singh took a detour through the town of Ka-erh on the Indus River. When he heard that people were saying he was a British spy, he and his companions hurried on their way. In 1867 they returned to India having successfully completed another expedition.

Voyage to Lhasa

After traveling with a diplomatic mission to Yarkand, Singh was asked to make a third and last expedition—to follow a route from the region of Ladakh through central Tibet to its capital, Lhasa. His ultimate goal was to travel with a Chinese caravan to Peking (now known as Beijing), China. Disguised as Buddhist monks, he and four companions traveled with a flock of sheep as additional cover. The mission lasted almost two years, from July 15, 1874, to March 1, 1876. Although they never reached Peking, the expedition gathered a great deal of information. They mapped mountain lakes and verified the existence of Tengri Nor, a large lake that Mani Singh had discovered three years before.

Nain Singh and his companions reached Lhasa in 1875 but stayed only two days. Singh did not receive some money he was expecting, and rumors about an approaching British agent were flying around the city. Fearing they would be detected, Singh sent the other two men to Leh in Kashmir with his astronomical survey. Singh himself headed for the fastest route to India, traveling through the Himalaya Mountains. When he entered the small Himalayan state of Tawang in December 1875, he was taken prisoner and held until February 1876. He managed to escape and reached British territory in March, sailing safely home via Calcutta.

Final years

Singh had achieved a successful career as a pundit, having completed all of his assignments in spite of obstacles. His loyalty to Great Britain never wavered, even though he frequently had to resort to bribery and trickery to complete his missions. His accomplishments were reported in the *Geo-*

graphical Magazine of the Royal Geographical Society in 1876. In 1877 the British government granted him a piece of land and a pension. He received a gold watch from the Paris Geographical Society and the coveted gold medal from the Royal Geographical Society.

Singh then helped to instruct other pundits. After he retired to his land, he led a quiet life. *The Times* of London reported his death in 1882 from cholera, but another report states that he died in 1895 from a heart attack. Although the circumstances of his death are uncertain, his contribution to British exploration and knowledge about Asia remains unchallenged.

Jedediah Smith

Born January 6, 1799,
Jericho, New York

Died May 27, 1831,
Near Santa Fe, New Mexico

Jedediah Smith's Trek across the Mojave Desert,
1826 by Frederic Remington, 1906 ▶

Jedediah Smith was one of the famed mountain men of the American West. He rediscovered the South Pass, which became the principal gateway for travelers to the Far West; he also pioneered the overland route to California and opened the overland route from California to the Columbia River. Later Smith became a partner in a prosperous fur-trading company. He was killed by Comanche Indians on the way to Santa Fe, New Mexico.

Takes job in fur trade

Jedediah Strong Smith was born on January 6, 1799, in Jericho, New York, to parents who had come from New Hampshire. The family moved to western Pennsylvania in either 1810 or 1811. In the spring of 1822 Smith went to St. Louis, Missouri, where he was hired by William Henry Ashley, a Virginia businessman who had founded a fur-trading company in the city. Smith went on Ashley's first expedition

Jedediah Smith, an American trapper and fur trader, was the first American to travel overland to the region that was once part of Mexico and is now the southwestern United States.

Mountain men

Jedediah Smith is considered the greatest of the mountain men, the name given to fur trappers and traders who roamed the Rocky Mountains during the 1820s and 1830s. Like Smith, most of them worked for William Henry Ashley's fur company, which—unlike the Hudson's Bay Company—had no permanent forts and conducted business by bartering with Native Americans. Known for their independence and resourcefulness, the mountain men prospered or perished on whatever they could hunt, trap, or fish. They learned survival skills from Native Americans and traveled in groups or alone in the wilderness hunting for furs.

The mountain men usually entered "civilization" once a year when they attended the fur traders' rendezvous, where they delivered their furs and received their yearly wages and supplies. Since they came to know the mountains, streams, rivers, and other features of the fur-rich country, they made many important geographical discoveries; they are also credited with opening the West to exploration and settlement. Once westward expansion began the mountain men were in demand as guides for expeditions and wagon trains. Among other well-known mountain men were James Bridger and Kit Carson.

to the West between 1822 and 1823 with the first large group of trappers to venture into that region.

In September 1823 Smith was put in charge of an expedition that left Fort Lookout on the upper Missouri River with plans to trap in the central Rockies and Columbia River areas. Smith led 11 men across the Great Plains via the White River and through the Badlands of the Dakotas and the Black Hills. While crossing the Badlands the party nearly died of thirst. In the Black Hills, Smith was attacked by a wounded grizzly bear that almost crushed his head between its jaws. One of Smith's men sewed up the wounds with a needle and thread and reattached his ear. After that incident Smith always wore his hair long to cover up the scars. During the ten days it took for him to recover, his men explored the Black Hills.

Pioneers mountain pass

Traveling across the Belle Fourche River, Smith and his men continued on into the Powder River Valley, over the Bighorn Mountains through Granite Pass, and into the basin of the Bighorn River. They spent the winter of 1823-24 at a Crow village in the Wind River Valley near present-day Dubois, Wyoming. They left in late February 1824, crossing the continental divide into the Green River valley in mid-March. The trail that they pioneered through the mountains was named South Pass; it later became the main passageway for Americans moving west. Once they reached the Green River and found it to be rich in beaver they divided into two parties to trap the length of the river.

In September 1824 Smith encountered a party of Native Americans who worked for the British Hudson's Bay Company. He and seven of his men traveled with them and their leader, Alexander Ross, to the company's Flathead Post in present-day Edy, Montana. Smith and his party spent the winter of 1824 there as unwelcome guests of the Hudson's Bay Company.

Becomes Ashley's partner

Smith had sent word back to Ashley about the rich fur country he had found. In early July 1825 Ashley traveled up the Missouri from St. Louis to meet Smith on the Green River. This was the first major rendezvous of fur trappers and traders that was to become an annual event for over 20 years. The following October Smith and Ashley took their large supply of furs back down the river to St. Louis, where Smith then concluded an agreement with Ashley to become his partner. A month later he headed back toward the Rocky Mountains. He had traveled only as far as the Platte River in western Nebraska when winter set in, so he was forced to winter in a village of the Pawnee tribe.

Smith and Ashley met again in the spring of 1826. At this meeting Ashley sold his interest in the fur-trading company he had founded to form a partnership that included Smith. Following the conclusion of this agreement, Smith headed toward the Great Salt Lake, which he had seen in 1824, in order to investigate reports that the lake was linked with the Pacific Ocean by the legendary Buenaventura River. He had already sent David Jackson with a small party to explore the area north and west of the lake, but they failed to find the Buenaventura, which in reality did not exist.

Blazes overland trail to California

In August 1826 Smith led his own party of 16 men from the Cache Valley to the Great Salt Lake and then to Utah Lake. They followed the Virgin River downstream to the Colorado River, where they stayed for two weeks as guests of the

Mojave tribe. They then crossed the Mojave Desert by following the course of the Mojave River, which Smith named the Inconstant. The party reached Mission San Gabriel in what is now a suburb of Los Angeles on November 27, 1826, becoming the first Americans to travel overland to California. This major achievement ultimately removed the obstacle to American settlement of California. Smith left his men and went to report to the Mexican governor of California in San Diego. The governor was not at all happy to see him and made him promise to return the way he had come. Booking passage on a United States trading ship from San Diego, Smith rejoined his men south of Los Angeles.

The Americans did not follow their original route on their return trip. They went north over the Tehachapi Mountains into the San Joaquin Valley in central California, where they were gratified to find the furs they had been looking for but did not locate the Buenaventura River. In May 1827 they tried to cross the Sierra Nevada range by following the American River near Sacramento; however, the snow was still too deep in the mountains and they were forced to turn back. Receiving word that the Mexican governor had sent troops after him, Smith led his men farther south up the Stanislaus River, where they were able to make it over the mountains to Walker Lake in what is now Nevada. They reached the Great Basin in time to participate in the trappers' rendezvous at Bear Lake in July. They were welcomed with cannon fire because they had long since been given up for lost.

Has problems with Native Americans and Mexicans

Smith and his men rested for only nine days before going back west. They reached the Mojave villages again in August. At first the Mojaves were quite friendly, as they had been during the previous visit. But as the trappers tried to cross the Colorado River the Native Americans attacked and killed half of the men in Smith's party. Smith and the other survivors escaped down the river on a raft, eventually reaching their former camp on the Stanislaus River. This time Smith and his companions were arrested by the Mexicans and taken to Monterey, the capital of the province of Alta California. They were held for two months before being released in late December. They reached the Umpqua River in southern Oregon in mid-July of the following year.

Smith's aim was to find the Willamette River, which he knew flowed into the Columbia. He left with two companions on the morning of July 14 to scout the best route. While they were away a band from the Umpqua tribe attacked the rest of the party, killing all but one man, who was able to escape into the woods and rejoin Smith. The four survivors made their way up the coast to the Hudson's Bay Company's headquarters at Fort Vancouver, Washington, across the Columbia River from Portland, Oregon. The British sent out a party to punish the Native Americans and bought the furs that Smith had been able to salvage. Smith stayed at Fort Vancouver until March 12, 1829. He did not get back to the Rockies in time to take part in the 1829 trappers' rendezvous and auction.

Plans to open new trade route

During the following winter Smith trapped in the Blackfoot country of what is now western Montana. In July 1830 he went to the fur rendezvous along the Wind River, where he and his partners sold their fur-trade to a new group of traders who also called themselves the Rocky Mountain Fur Company. Using the profits from the sale to buy a farm and a townhouse, Smith returned to St. Louis. There he became interested in a plan to open a trading route between the United States and Santa Fe, New Mexico.

In April 1831 Smith led a wagon train from St. Louis. A month later they came upon the dry stretch of land between the Arkansas and Cimarron rivers in southern Kansas. After the party had gone three days without water, Smith went ahead to look for a water source. He was never seen again. When the rest of the wagon train arrived at Santa Fe, they found Smith's pistols and rifle, which had been traded by a group of Comanches who had killed him at a water hole near the Cimarron River. The legendary and colorful mountain man was only 32 years old when he died.

John Smith

Born January 1580,
Willoughby, Lincolnshire, England

Died June, 1631,
London, England

John Smith, an English explorer, helped establish Jamestown, the first permanent English settlement in America. He explored Chesapeake Bay and the coast of the region. His books and maps contributed greatly to English knowledge of the New World.

Even before he reached North America, John Smith had led a life full of adventure and danger. His legendary encounter with Pocahontas is just one of many exciting episodes found in several books he wrote about his own life. Smith's accounts of his adventures have not always been believed since they are quite flattering to him. There is no proof, however, that his stories are untrue.

Early years as a soldier

Smith's life as an explorer began early. He worked as a merchant's apprentice until his father died in 1596. Striking out on his own at the age of 16, he left his home in the English county of Lincolnshire to become a soldier. He first joined the French, who were at war with Spain; later he fought with the Dutch, who were revolting against their Spanish rulers. In 1600 he joined the army of Austria against the Ottoman Turks in eastern Europe. According to Smith, while with the Austrian army he was responsible for two great victories and single-handedly fought three Turkish warriors in a row. Impressed by Smith's bravery, Prince Sigismund Bathori of Transylvania (a region now part of Romania) granted him a coat of arms and an annual pension.

During subsequent fighting in Transylvania, Smith was taken prisoner by the Turks and was sent to Constantinople (the city that is present-day Istanbul). While in captivity he was given as a present to the wife of a Turkish military official. According to Smith, she fell in love with him and sent him to her brother in the port of Varna on the Black Sea for safekeeping. There he was enslaved and was forced to kill his master in order to escape. Returning to Transylvania, he received protection from Prince Sigismund.

Voyage to the New World

Following a trip to Morocco, Smith met an English naval ship and returned to his native country in 1605. His next plan was to join a group of colonizers who were going to Guiana, a region on the northeastern coast of South America. This scheme did not succeed, however, and instead Smith joined the New London Company, a group of 105 men who were going to establish the first permanent English settlement in America.

In April 1607, after a voyage of four months, they arrived along the coast of Virginia. The men had brought with them sealed instructions regarding their duties. When these instructions were opened, they revealed that Smith had been named one of the seven members of the governing council of the settlement, which was to be named Jamestown. Smith's appointment was ironic since he had caused trouble on the voyage and had been accused of conspiring to mutiny.

Leader of the Jamestown settlement

Once the colonists established themselves at Jamestown, however, Smith quickly proved himself as a leader. He took charge of exploring and mapping the surrounding territory and establishing trade relations with neighboring Native Americans in order to acquire necessities for the colonists. Smith guided the settlement through its first difficult years, during which 80 percent of the colonists died.

Smith's first trip into the wilderness took him up the James River as far as the site of present-day Richmond. On an expedition to the Chickahominy River in December 1607, he was captured by members of what the English called the Powhatan tribe. He was taken to the main camp of King Powhatan (whose real name was Wahunsenacawh). Smith was condemned to death by having his brains beaten out, but he was saved at the last minute by Powhatan's young daughter, Pocahontas. This famous story may or may not be true, but Pocahontas (whose real name was Matoaka) did exist. She later married another English settler, John Rolfe, and moved with him to England, where she eventually died from smallpox.

During the summer of 1608 Smith made two more major expeditions. He had received instructions from London to search for a passage westward from Chesapeake Bay to the Pacific Ocean. Smith sent back his accounts of these explorations in a work called the *True Relation of ... Virginia,* written in July 1608, as well as in *A Map of Virginia,* drawn in 1612. These documents gave the English their first knowledge of the area that was to become Virginia and Maryland.

Search for the Pacific Ocean

On his first attempt to find a passage to the Pacific, Smith and his companions traveled up the coast of Chesapeake Bay as far as the Patapsco River, where Baltimore now stands. On their return they went up the Potomac River as far as the site of present-day Washington, D.C., taking a detour up the Rappahanock River. At this point Smith was seriously injured. While spearing fish for food, he was stung by a stingray, a marine fish related to the shark. His body was so swollen and his fever so high that his companions thought he was going to die. Smith recovered, however, and the spot where he was injured has been called Stingray Point ever since.

The goal of Smith's second expedition was to travel all the way up Chesapeake Bay. His party reached the Patapsco within two days, and from there they explored the mouth of the Susquehannah and other rivers that flow into the north end of the bay. Finding a waterfall on the Susquehannah, Smith named it after himself. Smith also explored the Patuxent, Rappahannock, and Nansemond rivers.

During their explorations the men encountered two previously unknown groups of Native Americans, the Massawomekes and the Tockwoughs. Smith also met a party of Susquahannock traders, who came from an Iroquois tribe unrelated to the Algonquins he had previously known. The Susquahannocks had European goods that Smith rightly guessed had been obtained by trading with the French. During the winter of 1608-09 Smith served as president of the council that governed Virginia. He saved the colony by bartering with the Native Americans for corn. After being badly injured in an accidental gunpowder explosion, Smith returned to England. During his recovery he promoted the settling of North America, although he himself was never to return to Virginia.

Exploration of New England

In March 1614 Smith was sent by a group of London merchants to explore the region north of Virginia and to report back on its prospects for settlement. He returned to England with a valuable cargo of furs and fish, and he used his new knowledge to write *A Description of New England* in 1616. This book was the first English work to show the contours of New England. In fact, it was in this work that Smith gave the region its name. He also used several other names, including Plymouth, that were kept by the later Puritan settlers.

Impressed by Smith's accomplishments, a wealthy English merchant, Sir Ferdinando Gorges, sent him on two additional voyages of exploration. Neither was successful. On the first trip Smith was forced to turn back when his ship lost its mast in a storm. He set out again and was captured first by pirates and then by a French naval ship. After helping the French fight the Spanish, Smith was released in the French port of La Rochelle. He tried to sail to America once more in 1617 but was forced to turn back because of bad weather.

Smith spent the rest of his life in London, writing pamphlets about North America, drawing maps, and recounting his adventures. Though he may have embellished some of his stories, there is no question that he played an important role in the early settlement of the English colonies.

Hernando de Soto

Born c. 1500,
Extremadura, Spain
Died May 21, 1542,
Mississippi River

By 1539, when his expedition sailed along the coast of Florida, Hernando de Soto was already a seasoned explorer and a wealthy man. He had been drawn to the North American continent by stories about hidden cities that contained vast amounts of gold and silver. De Soto and his party, who traveled for nearly three years in search of treasure, were possibly the first Europeans to sight the Mississippi River.

Born in about 1500 in Extremadura, a Spanish province near the Portuguese border, de Soto embarked on a life of adventure as a young man. In 1524 he joined an expedition to Nicaragua led by Francisco Hernandez de Córdoba, taking part in founding the city of Granada. Sometime after their arrival in Nicaragua, de Soto sided with Córdoba's adversary, Pedro Arias, in a dispute that resulted in Córdoba's death. De Soto settled in Nicaragua and began to prosper, partly by engaging in slave trade. Once again lured by adventure, however, he accepted an invitation to join fellow Spaniard **Francisco Pizarro** (see entry) in Pizarro's third expedition to Peru.

Hernando de Soto, a Spanish explorer, led the first European expedition into what is now the southeastern United States. He died along the way.

Conquest of Peru

When the Spaniards landed in Peru in December 1531, they began the conquest of the Inca Empire. With its capital at Cuzco, the empire extended thousands of miles throughout the region. The Spaniards traveled for nearly a year in the Andes, the great South American mountain range. In November 1532 they reached the city of Cajamarca, where Atahualpa, the ruler of the Incas, was camped. Pizarro sent de Soto into the city to meet Atahualpa. The next day Pizarro, pretending to be friendly, invited Atahualpa to dinner and then took him captive.

Having imprisoned Atahualpa, Pizarro became the ruler of Peru. Although there were several uprisings by the Incas, Pizarro stayed in power. During one of the revolts he ordered the execution of Atahualpa. In spite of de Soto's protests that the life of the emperor should be spared, the execution was carried out. The following year, in 1533, de Soto joined Pizarro in taking Cuzco, the capital. During the siege de Soto nearly lost his life in an ambush. He stayed in Peru for three more years before returning to Spain in 1536.

De Soto's participation in the conquest of Peru made him a man of wealth and stature. Upon his arrival in Spain, he asked King Charles I to give him an important position in one of Spain's new territories in the Americas. In April 1537 the king appointed de Soto governor of Cuba. As governor, de Soto was granted the right to conquer and colonize the territory north of Cuba on the mainland of North America, later to become Florida. This land, first visited by **Juan Ponce de León** (see entry) in 1513, was at the time a vast, unexplored wilderness.

Expedition to Florida

De Soto began preparing for an expedition to Florida. In the meantime, **Álvar Núñez Cabeza de Vaca** (see entry) returned to Spain after many years of exploring in the area that is now Texas. Cabeza de Vaca told of stories he had heard about the great wealth to be found in the "Seven Cities of Cíbola," which were said to be somewhere in the southeastern part of North America. While Cabeza de Vaca had failed to find any

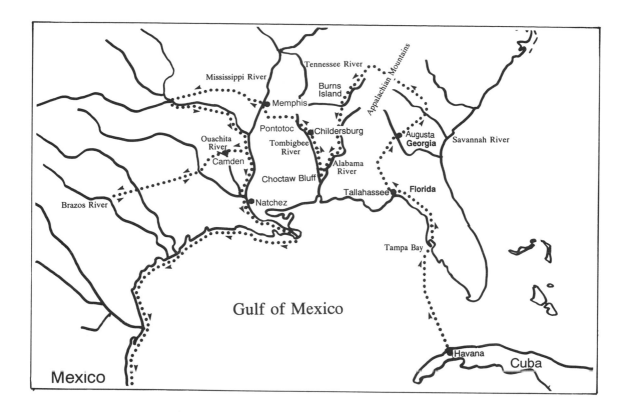

treasure, de Soto felt encouraged that he himself might discover riches in his new territory. He sailed from Spain on April 7, 1538, with 600 men and 200 horses. After stopping in Cuba for more supplies, they landed at the site of modern-day Tampa Bay, on the western coast of Florida, on May 27, 1539.

Six months later de Soto and his party reached the town of Apalachen near what is now Tallahassee, Florida. In spite of a hostile reception from Native Americans, they spent the winter there. When spring came, they left in search of a place called Cofitachequi, which they had heard was ruled by a powerful and wealthy queen. They arrived at Cofitachequi, about 75 miles from the mouth of the Savannah River in eastern Georgia, in late April 1540. The city was indeed ruled by a queen, but her only treasure was a few freshwater pearls.

De Soto´s party explored nearly all of the southeastern area of the United States in a futile attempt to find treasure.

Battle with Native Americans

The expedition left Cofitachequi two weeks later and

moved north to the land of Chiaha, also rumored to be rich in gold. In early June, after crossing the Appalachian Mountains, they reached Chiaha, which turned out to be an island (now named Burns Island) in the middle of the Tennessee River. Once again, promises of wealth proved to be false. From there the disappointed Spaniards traveled south, on the way meeting two great chiefs—Chief Cosa, who lived along the Coosa River north of modern Childersburg, Alabama, and Chief Tuscaloosa, who lived in a village on the shores of the Alabama River.

At Mabila (perhaps near present-day Choctaw Bluff, Alabama) de Soto received news that his ships had sailed into the Gulf of Mexico to meet him. Moving down toward the gulf in November 1540, the de Soto party became involved in a fierce battle with a group of Native Americans. They were therefore diverted to the north and west and were forced to set up winter camp about 125 miles east of the Mississippi River. In March of the following year they were attacked by members of the Chickasaw tribe; 12 Spaniards were killed.

De Soto and his men left their winter camp at the end of April 1541 and reached the Mississippi in early May at a site that is south of modern Memphis, Tennessee. They built barges and crossed the river in June, again in search of treasure. De Soto had heard reports about the Ozark Mountains, so he headed in that direction with hopes of finding gold and silver. The party spent several months traveling through what is now the state of Arkansas, making a winter camp near Camden. They left camp on March 6, 1542, but by then they were in desperate straits. Juan Ortiz, an important member of the expedition, had died along with several other men and most of the horses. De Soto decided to turn back and sail down the Mississippi to the sea.

Death on the Mississippi

The party reached the river and pillaged a Native American village in order to have a secure place to build their boats. In the meantime, however, de Soto became ill with fever and died during the night of May 21, 1542. His men reportedly buried his body in the river so it would not be discovered by the Native Americans.

The survivors, led by Luis de Moscoso, built seven barges and embarked down the Brazos River in July. They reached the mouth of the Mississippi and then sailed along the Gulf coast to the settlement of Panuco in northwestern Mexico, where they would set sail for Spain. It was now September 10, 1543. Of the original 600 men in the de Soto expedition, only 311 had survived, and their leader had died without ever finding treasure in his new territory.

John Hanning Speke

Born May 4, 1827,
Ilminster, Somerset, England

Died September 16, 1864,
Bath, England

◀ *John Hanning Speke and James Augustus Grant*

John Hanning Speke, an English explorer, discovered the source of the Nile River at Lake Victoria in East Africa.

John Hanning Speke was at the center of one of the biggest geographical controversies of the nineteenth century—the search for the source of the Nile River in East Africa. The controversy would pit Speke against fellow explorer **Richard Burton** (see entry), and each man would pay a heavy price for his involvement. The two men were opposites in temperament and interests, and their differences added to the dislike each held for the other.

Speke was born in the town of Ilminster in Somerset County, England, on May 4, 1827. His father, an army officer, prepared his son for a life in the military. At age 17 Speke entered the British army in India and fought in several campaigns there. He was promoted to lieutenant in 1850, when he was 23, and then to captain two years later. During his time in India, Speke developed an interest in hunting and exploring, taking treks to the Himalayas and Tibet. After concluding his ten-year tour of duty in India, Speke traveled to the British colony of Aden on the southern coast of Arabia.

First expedition with Burton

It was in Aden that Speke met Burton, and this meeting would in time change both men's lives. Speke signed up for Burton's expedition to Somaliland on the northeastern coast of Africa. Before heading south the explorers made camp at Berbera on the coast of the Red Sea. Somali warriors attacked Burton's party, taking everyone by surprise. Speke sustained 11 wounds, some of them serious; he was captured but then managed to escape. A javelin pierced Burton's jaw, but he miraculously survived.

Upon returning to England to recover from his injuries, Speke volunteered for service in the Crimean War (fought mostly on Russia's Crimea Peninsula), which Great Britain had entered in 1854. After the war Speke was thinking about further explorations when he was invited by Burton to join him on a new expedition to East Africa (now divided into the countries of Kenya, Tanzania, and Uganda) to try to find Lake Nyasa. They arrived on the island of Zanzibar off the coast of Africa on December 21. Faced with the dilemma of which direction to take, Burton spent six months reaching the conclusion that the caravan route from Unyanyembe to Bagamoyo was best. They set out from the coast of East Africa on June 27, 1857, accompanied by a great caravan of porters and supplies led by **Sidi Mubarak Bombay** (see entry), the freed African slave who served many European explorers.

Malaria and high fever

Burton and Speke's caravan proceeded slowly, taking 134 days to reach Tabora in western Tanzania. Porters deserted the caravan and took the party's food with them. Even worse than the desertions was the health of Speke and Burton; both men were suffering from malaria and high fever. Speke temporarily lost his sight from ophthalmia. Often too ill to walk, the explorers had to be carried in hammocks. The rugged terrain, coupled with their poor health, made the trip almost impossible. In late July they reached the important caravan station of Zungomero, where they rested and where Burton recruited new porters for the next leg of the journey.

During this five-week interlude, differences between the two men because obvious. Burton quickly made friends with the local Arabs by demonstrating his knowledge of the Koran and by acting out scenes from the *Arabian Nights,* to the enjoyment of everyone except Speke. Since he did not have Burton's intellectual ability or flamboyance, Speke limited his interests to big-game hunting, which Burton disliked.

The explorers joined an Arab caravan at Ugogo and traveled to Kazeh—the modern Tanzanian city of Tabora—which they reached on November 7. While they were in Kazeh, they learned that the "Lake Nyasa" they were searching for was actually one of three great interior lakes. They were led to believe that one of these lakes was the source of the Nile, the longest river in the world, which flows 4,187 miles from its headstream, the Luvironza, in Africa to the Mediterranean Sea.

Search for the Nile's source

Excited by the prospect of locating the long-sought source of the Nile, the two explorers set out again on December 5, although Burton was so ill with fever that he had to be carried in a litter, and Speke was half-blind with an eye infection. On February 13, 1858, they reached Lake Tanganyika, the world's longest freshwater lake, on the boundary between Zaire and Tanzania. Upon viewing the lake from a hilltop, Burton wrote in his diary that it was "an expanse of the lightest and softest blue, in breadth varying from thirty to thirty-two miles."

In the lakeside village of Ujiji, Burton learned that a river named Rusizi was at the lake's head. Burton and Speke reasoned that if the Rusizi flowed outward, they had found the source of the Nile. Before reaching the northern end of the lake, the canoe paddlers, fearing hostile tribes, deserted the two men. Burton, whose tongue was ulcerated, was in too much pain to travel without help. Even though natives said the river flowed inward, Burton was unable to verify the fact himself, so he did not abandon his belief that he had found the Nile's source. Speke, however, had his doubts.

Speke and Burton returned to Tabora near the end of June 1858. By that time they were no longer on speaking terms. Speke wanted to explore a lake north of Tabora while Burton was recovering. To get rid of Speke, Burton agreed to the plan. On August 3 Speke reached the vast lake, which he named Lake Victoria after the queen of England. His calculations and other indications convinced him he had found the source of the Nile. He returned to Tabora on August 25, 1858, and told Burton the news. Burton refused to believe his partner had found the source of the Nile. Their arguments became even more intense because Speke's discovery was more than Burton could tolerate. Burton refused to recognize that his own lifelong dream had been realized by a man he considered to be his inferior. Speke urged Burton to go with him to see Lake Victoria, but Burton refused.

Speke and Burton left Tabora on September 6. The return trip to the coast was painful and difficult. Delirious and suffering from his worst case of malaria thus far, Speke denounced Burton. His hatred of Burton was not limited to their dispute over the Nile—he did not approve of Burton's morals. Speke was also upset over his belief that Burton thought he had been a coward at Berbera. Speke also felt slighted by Burton's having relegated Speke's diary to an appendix in his book, *First Steps in Africa*. When Speke was well enough to travel, he had to be transported in a hammock aboard the ship they were taking to Aden, where they planned to recuperate. Speke left a few days later, however, after promising Burton he would not make a report to the Royal Geographical Society until they could do it together.

Return to Lake Victoria

Speke broke his word to Burton. Two days after arriving in London, he spoke to the Royal Geographical Society. His news about the discovery of the source of the Nile was enthusiastically received in England. The Royal Geographical Society immediately made plans to send him out again to confirm his discovery. Burton's career thus was effectively over. Speke left England on April 27, 1860, this time accompanied by James

Augustus Grant, a Scotsman and fellow big-game hunter. Speke's plan was to travel from Zanzibar to Tabora and then north to Lake Victoria, inspecting the north shore and entering the White Nile at its source. Speke's last communication to England was dated September 30, 1861; no one heard from him for more than a year. In the meantime, the Royal Geographical Society sent John Petherick, the British consul at Khartoum, south down the Nile with a load of supplies to meet Speke as he was coming from the north. Petherick, who also was not heard from for several months, was presumed dead.

Speke had, in fact, traveled from Tabora back to Lake Victoria and moved around the western end of the lake, carefully mapping the northwestern shore. Along the way he met the rulers of several African kingdoms—Karagwe, Buganda, and Bunyoro. Speke found the source of the Nile River on July 28, 1862, when he stood at a large waterfall that was 12 feet tall and 700 yards wide and surrounded by crocodiles and hippopotamuses. He named the waterfall Ripon Falls after the president of the Royal Geographical Society. Speke was not able to follow the Nile's course northward because of hostile tribes and the famine there, a fact his critics would later use against him. On February 15, 1863, he and Grant reached Gondokoro, a town on the right bank of the White Nile.

Speke expected to meet Petherick at Gondokoro but instead was greeted by the explorers **Samuel White Baker** and his future wife **Florence** (see combined entry), who were traveling south on the Nile and also searching for the river's source. Petherick and his wife had gone big-game hunting because they had grown tired of waiting for Speke, who was expected to arrive months earlier. Speke did not like this turn of events and therefore regarded Petherick as an enemy like Burton.

Renewed debate with Burton

Upon his return to England, Speke was welcomed as a hero. But soon he became involved in controversy. First, the Royal Geographical Society had to clear Petherick of charges Speke had brought against him as a result of the incident in

Gondokoro. Speke further alienated the society when he refused to permit publication of his findings in its journal, favoring a commercial publisher instead. At the same time, geographers were raising questions about Speke's accuracy in pinpointing the Nile's source. When Burton returned to England in 1864, he renewed his dispute with Speke. Burton contended that by not following the river for all of its distance, Speke had not proved that the river flowing out of Lake Victoria was actually the Nile.

In an attempt to resolve the matter, the British Association for the Advancement of Science scheduled a public debate, with **David Livingstone** (see entry) as referee, on September 16, 1864, so that Burton and Speke could argue their positions. Burton and the audience were already assembled when it was announced that Speke had died earlier in a hunting accident. Because Speke was an experienced gunman who was hunting alone and because the investigation into his death was incomplete, the suspicion of suicide remains strong. Speke's claim that he had found the source of the Nile at Lake Victoria was ultimately proved to be correct.

Sputnik

Launched October 4, 1957
Decommissioned March 25, 1961

The Soviet Union's Sputnik program produced the first spacecraft to orbit Earth.

At the height of the Cold War the Soviet Union initiated a space program named *Sputnik*, which made such historic achievements as putting the first satellite in Earth's orbit; it prepared the way for sending the first human aboard a spacecraft into Earth's orbit. In 1955 the Soviet Union began construction of the Baikonur Space Center in Kazakhstan near the town of Tyuratam. One of the top priorities at the new base was the *A-1*, the first intercontinental ballistic missile (ICBM). Launched on August 3, 1957, the *A-1* missile traveled a distance of 5,000 miles, thus laying the foundation for the first artificial satellite. On September 18, 1957, the Soviet Union announced its intention to launch a satellite but withheld its name—*Sputnik*, which means traveling companion.

Soviets launch space age

Both the *A-1* and *Sputnik* were designed by the Soviet Union's premier space engineer, Sergei Korolov. Nothing was

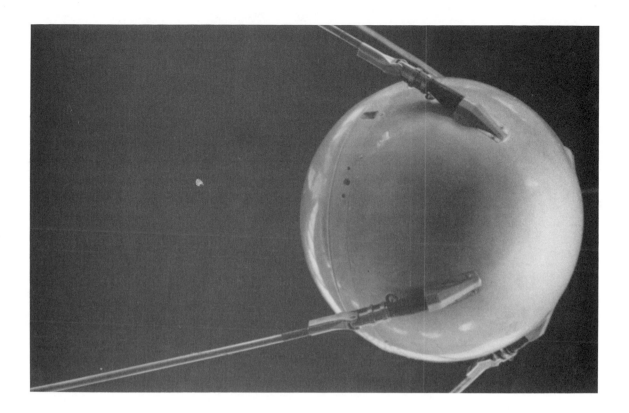

known about Korolov in the West, and the envious Americans called him the "Chief Designer." He had been imprisoned twice during Joseph Stalin's rule but had survived to become the moving force behind the Soviet space program under Nikita Khrushchev. Korolov's name was not made public until his death in January 1966. The Soviet Union launched the first *Sputnik* on October 4, 1957, one of the great dates in history because it marked the first time humans were able to successfully send an object beyond Earth's atmosphere. The event was the beginning of the space age.

Sputnik 1 made 4,000 trips around Earth before it gradually lost altitude and disintegrated as it reentered denser atmosphere.

Sputnik 1 makes history

Sputnik 1 was essentially a 184-pound radio transmitter enclosed in a steel case with four antennas sticking out of it. The satellite's instruments were designed to study the density, temperature, and concentration of electrons in the upper atmosphere and to transmit the results back to Earth. It took 95 minutes to circle Earth in an elliptical orbit—the altitude varied from about 140 to 560 miles. *Sputnik 1* made about 4,000 trips around Earth before gradually losing altitude and disintegrating as it re-entered denser atmosphere on January 4, 1958.

United States reacts with alarm

The world was impressed with the Soviet Union's accomplishment, especially since much of the country had been devastated by the Stalinist dictatorship and World War II. The space program had started only after the Great Patriotic War, as World War II is called in the Soviet Union. The reaction in the United States was alarmist, however: the launch occurred at the height of the cold war, and Americans saw it as a major victory for their adversaries. A Congressional investigation questioned why the United States had fallen behind, and the public demanded results quickly. This national shock caused two reactions—the formation of the National Aeronautics and Space Administration (NASA) in July 1958 and a renewed emphasis on teaching science in U.S. schools.

Sputnik 2 carries passenger

The relatively simple technology of *Sputnik 1* was quickly followed by sophisticated advancements. The Soviets launched *Sputnik 2* less than a month later, on November 3, 1957. It was much bigger, weighing 1,120 pounds, and it flew at a much higher altitude. More impressively, the spacecraft carried a passenger, a female dog named Laika. Obviously, Laika's flight was intended to test the possibility of sending humans into space. Laika suffered no ill effects from weightlessness and was able to move about and eat food. Unfortunately, the oxygen in Laika's cabin gave out after a week and she died. *Sputnik 2* stayed in orbit for 163 days before disintegrating in April 1958.

Sputniks 3 and *4* make advances

Sputnik 3, launched a month later, was much larger than its two predecessors, weighing a ton and a half. The spacecraft contained various instruments for measuring the pressure and composition of the upper atmosphere, the incidence of micro-meteoroids, and solar and cosmic radiation. In effect, *Sputnik 3* was a miniature science lab and was even equipped with an onboard computer. It stayed in orbit for 691 days.

After *Sputnik 3* the Soviets began making plans to put a human into space, as was clearly indicated by *Sputnik 4*. Launched two years later, on May 15, 1960, the spacecraft was the first of the *Vostok* series, which contained a cabin and an ejector seat for the cosmonaut on board. It carried a dummy passenger, which was fortunate because it went off course four days after launching and swung into a high orbit until it disintegrated in October 1965.

Sputniks 5 and *6* continue passenger tests

The aim of the Soviet flights was to successfully send a spacecraft into orbit and then to change its path and bring it safely back to Earth, a feat that had not yet been accomplished. *Sputnik 5* achieved this goal. Sent into space on August 19, 1960, the craft carried two dogs named Belka and Strelka as well as two rats and 28 mice. The day after launch, *Sputnik 5*'s descent cabin separated and headed back to Earth. Two cabins containing the two dogs were ejected and came down to the ground, slowed by parachutes. Wary farmers in a field recovered Strelka and Belka, who were both alive and well.

Soviet scientists concluded it was possible to send a human into space safely. *Sputnik 6* was launched on December 1, 1960, with two dogs, Pchelka and Mushka, on board; it was to be the last scheduled trial flight in the *Sputnik* series. Two days later the rockets fired to change orbit, but the angle of descent was too steep and the spacecraft burned up. More test flights would be needed.

Final trials lead to human in space

Sputniks 7 and 8 were actually the first Soviet probes of the planet Venus, later known as the *Venera* project. Although *Sputnik 7* successfully reached Earth orbit, ground control failed to redirect it toward Venus. *Sputnik 8* headed into the proper orbit but its communications equipment failed and all contact was lost. *Sputnik 9*, which was sent up on March 9, 1961, and *Sputnik 10*, which was launched on March 25, were both successful. They both carried dogs—Chernushka on *Sputnik 9* and Zvedochka on *Sputnik 10*—into orbit and returned them safely to Earth. It was now time to send the first human into space. Again the Soviet Union achieved a space-age first, gaining world attention: on April 5, 1961, **Yury Gagarin** (see entry) made his historic flight aboard the *Vostok* to become the first human to circle Earth in a spacecraft.

Hester Stanhope

Born March 12, 1776,
Kent, England
Died June 23, 1839,
Mount Lebanon, Lebanon

H ester Stanhope spent most of her adult life living a romantic dream of travel and adventure in the Middle East. Highly intelligent, she was an independent woman with a flair for the dramatic and a never-ending curiosity about the world around her. During her lifetime she ventured into areas that few Europeans had ever seen, a fact made even more remarkable because she was living at a time when women had few rights or privileges. Stanhope adopted the dress of a Turkish gentleman and for a time was the absolute monarch of her own tiny kingdom. She gradually cut all ties with the Western world, dying penniless and alone in 1839.

Born on March 12, 1776, Hester Lucy Stanhope had a lonely and unhappy childhood. Her father was the third earl of Stanhope, and her mother was the favorite sister of Sir William Pitt, who became prime minister of Great Britain in 1783. Stanhope's father, however, was a political radical and inventor whose many interests left little time for his children. Stanhope's education was therefore erratic and haphazard. She

Lady Hester Stanhope, a flamboyant, unconventional English noblewoman, spent much of her life traveling through the Middle East.

was only four years old when her mother died; she then went to live with her grandmother until her death in 1803.

Early life in Pitt's household

After the death of Stanhope's grandmother, her famous bachelor uncle, Sir William Pitt, invited her to manage his household. The Pitt family had been at the center of English politics for many years, and Pitt's friends were wealthy and powerful. Undaunted by her new surroundings, Stanhope soon developed a reputation for doing and saying exactly what she pleased. Her uncle's friends were sometimes shocked by her actions, but Pitt loyally defended her.

Stanhope eventually served as Pitt's hostess, arranged banquets, and handled his correspondence, and she was his most trusted adviser until he died unexpectedly in 1806. He left Stanhope with a small inheritance but no other prospects. When a friend had once remarked to Pitt that his niece would marry when she found a man as clever as herself, Pitt replied, "Then she will never marry at all."

In fact, Stanhope never did marry. She was courted, however, by Sir John Moore, a prominent general in the English army, before he went to fight in the war against France in northern Spain. But Moore was killed on January 16, 1809, at the Battle of Coruña, where the British army was pitted against the army of Napoléon Bonaparte. Moore died in the arms of Stanhope's brother, James; his last words were "Stanhope, remember me to your sister." Later that same day Stanhope's favorite brother, Charles, died in battle after being shot through the heart. Overcome with grief, Stanhope lived for a short time in a cottage in Wales before deciding to leave her unhappiness behind and escape the restrictions of conventional English society. She set sail for a trip to the Mediterranean and never saw England again.

Voyage across the Continent

Stanhope's traveling party included a Welsh female companion; her personal physician, Dr. Charles Meryon; and an entourage of servants. Although apparently never romantically involved with Stanhope, Meryon accompanied her on her travels for many years and wrote two books about their adventures. After visiting Stanhope's brother in Gibraltar, they sailed to the island of Malta, where Stanhope formed a liaison with a young Scottish nobleman named Michael Bruce. He was 23 years old, and she was 34. Since Bruce was dependent on his family for an income, Stanhope proposed writing to his father and asking for his approval of their arrangement. The senior Bruce's reply to Stanhope began, "Our correspondence has certainly started off on a very extraordinary footing." But he accepted the liaison and, in effect, agreed to finance it, thinking Michael Bruce could learn from his experiences with Stanhope.

After leaving Malta Stanhope decided she wanted to go to Constantinople (now Istanbul) in Turkey, where she planned to meet the French ambassador, who she hoped would arrange an introduction to Napoléon. Along the way she stopped in Athens, Greece, and met the English romantic poet Lord Byron. In November 1810 Stanhope and her party reached Constantinople, where she quickly became a celebrity. She shocked Turkish society when she appeared in a pair of overalls to inspect a Turkish warship.

She sailed from Constantinople in October 1811, heading for Alexandria in Egypt. Along the way the ship was wrecked in a storm; having nearly drowned, Stanhope and her friends were thrown up on the island of Rhodes. Since she had lost her clothes in the shipwreck, Stanhope adopted the dress of a Turkish gentleman, which was the costume she wore for the rest of her life.

In February 1812 Stanhope and her entourage traveled on to Egypt, where she was received by the khedive of Egypt at

Romanticism

Stanhope's decision to abandon conventional life was possibly influenced by a philosophical and artistic movement known as romanticism, which was flourishing in Europe during the late 1700s. Formulated by the French philosopher Jean Jacques Rousseau, romanticism idealized the so-called natural man, who was supposedly unspoiled by the corruption and luxury of civilization. Rousseau stressed freedom of the individual. Rejecting accepted social norms, he called for a return to nature, emulation of common people, and travel to remote and faraway places. These ideas, which influenced painting, music, drama, literature, and politics of the time, had tremendous appeal to the upper classes in England.

his palace in Cairo and visited the pyramids. She continued on to the Holy Land, passed through Jerusalem, and then joined a magnificent caravan traveling north to Acre, a city in Israel. By this time Stanhope's extravagance was beginning to become a burden on Bruce's father—he had paid the modern-day equivalent of $100,000 for their expenses over the previous eight months—and he refused to send any more money. The couple then broke up, and Bruce returned to England; he later became a lawyer and member of Parliament from Scotland.

Unconventional behavior

Stanhope continued to be a celebrity wherever she went. Her flamboyant personality and generosity must have fascinated her hosts, for she was able to do things and visit places that had previously been forbidden to Europeans. Once she was invited into the mountains of Lebanon to meet the emir of the Druses, who were at that time a little-known and mysterious Islamic sect. Stanhope was the first European admitted to the emir's palace. She again defied convention when she visited Bedouin tribes in the desert of what is now Jordan.

One of her more interesting adventures occurred at the ruins of the city of Palmyra in Syria. Palmyra had been ruled by another famous woman, Zenobia, a warrior queen who had defeated Roman armies and ruled Egypt until she was defeated in A.D. 270. When Stanhope expressed a desire to visit the city, which had been a main caravan stop in the days of the Roman Empire, she was cautioned that Westerners were not welcome. Ignoring the warnings, she rode into the Muslim city on a horse, not only without a veil covering her face but also dressed in men's clothing. Local residents came out to greet her; a child hung down from an arch and dropped a wreath on her head as though she were a queen visiting from a foreign land. On another outing Stanhope became the first European, male or female, to visit a harem and also the first to write about the visit.

Stanhope's castle in Lebanon

In May 1813 Stanhope went from Palmyra to the Mediterranean coast, where she settled in the Syrian port of

Latakia. She and Meryon became seriously ill when an epidemic of plague broke out, but they both survived. In the following years Stanhope and Meryon traveled along the eastern shore of the Mediterranean Sea, an area then called the Levant. They visited Roman ruins in Baalbek, Lebanon, and Ashquelon, Israel, as well as other archaeological sites.

When Meryon returned to England in 1817, Stanhope decided to live in Lebanon with the Druses. The emir of Acre ceded to her the ruins of a convent and the village of Dahar-June. She built a group of houses surrounded by a garden and outer wall. It looked like a medieval fortress, and she ruled in isolated splendor. The Druses admired Stanhope's courage and concern for the poor. For a time they venerated her as a kind of prophet. She adopted Eastern manners and customs, and Eastern ideas influenced her concepts of religion and philosophy. She continued to have contact with England through Meryon, who came frequently. Having become highly critical of English politics, Stanhope loved to argue with other distinguished Europeans who visited her. She entertained at her own whim, sometimes refusing to see people who had traveled hundreds of miles to call on her.

Stanhope was famous for her lavish hospitality, but her living habits were expensive. She had no way of paying her debts, and her creditors became increasingly insistent about collecting their money. As time went on she became more and more isolated, yet she still ruled over her little kingdom. Finally, in 1838 she simply shut herself up in her castle and refused to see anyone. She died alone the following year at the age of 63, proud and determined to control her own destiny to the end.

Henry Morton Stanley

Born 1841,
Denbigh, Wales
Died May 9, 1904,
London, England

Welsh-born Sir Henry Morton Stanley led an expedition to central Africa sponsored by an American newspaper to find the missing David Livingstone. He also led three other expeditions, tracing the course of the Congo River and exploring the great lakes of central Africa.

C onsidered the greatest of all African explorers, Henry Morton Stanley led a life of adventure and daring, and had a flare for being in the middle of controversy. Henry Morton Stanley was not his real name—he was born John Rowlands in Denbigh, Wales, in 1841, one of five children his mother bore out of wedlock. He lived with his grandfather until the age of six when, upon his grandfather's death, Rowlands was sent to St. Asaph Union Workhouse. At 17 Rowlands secured a job as cabin boy and jumped ship in New Orleans to escape the brutality on board. When Rowlands was adopted by a New Orleans cotton merchant named Henry Morton Stanley in 1859, the young man took his benefactor's name and nationality.

Has many adventures

Stanley was forced to join the Confederate army at the outbreak of the American Civil War. After being captured by

Union soldiers at the battle of Shiloh, he was released on the condition that he enlist in the Union army; he complied but then he became ill and received a medical discharge. Stanley served two years in the U.S. Merchant Marine before becoming a clerk in the Union navy. Near the end of the war he deserted and with Lewis Noe went to the mining camps of the American West. Stanley then persuaded Noe to go with him to Turkey to seek their fortunes. Both men were nearly killed by Turks in 1866.

After returning to the United States Stanley turned to journalism. He began his career as a reporter for the *Missouri Democrat,* covering General Hancock's campaigns against the Cheyenne and meeting such western figures as Wild Bill Hickok and George Armstrong Custer. James Gordon Bennett, Jr., owner of the New York *Herald,* hired Stanley to cover the British campaign in Abyssinia; in Alexandria Stanley bribed a telegraph operator to send his copy first to London after the British defeat of Theodore at Magdala. The cable between Malta and Alexandria then broke and Stanley's story scooped his competition by two weeks—he was famous.

Sent to find Livingstone

Bennett thought the person who found the explorer **David Livingstone** (see entry) in the interior of Africa would have the story of the century. Livingstone had headed an expedition in 1866 to continue the search for the sources of the Nile River. By 1868 no one had heard from him, and it was feared he might be dead. The Royal Geographical Society in London prepared an expedition to search for Livingstone, but letters written by Livingstone from the shores of Lake Nyasa arrived in Zanzibar, and the search was called off. Livingstone was noted for sending news of his progress back regularly; so when no further messages were received, Bennett decided news of Livingstone's whereabouts would give a boost to the newspaper's circulation, and he sent Stanley out to try to find him. "If he is dead bring back every possible proof of his death," Bennett said.

Stanley arrived in Zanzibar off the coast of East Africa at the beginning of 1871. Since the newspaper had provided him with unlimited funds, he used the money lavishly to equip the most expensive expedition ever to travel to the interior of Africa. He hired the veteran **Sidi Mubarak Bombay** (see entry) as caravan leader, departing on February 6, 1871. Stanley was a fast learner and quickly mastered the skills of a professional explorer. He was also a hard taskmaster, refusing to rest whatever the cost. When his two British assistants came down with fever, Stanley would not stop to rest; within six months the men had died.

It took Stanley two months to cover the 212 miles to the trading center of Kazeh, now modern Tabora in central Tanzania. Desertion and disease had depleted Stanley's ranks, and he had to hire more porters. At Tabora, Stanley found himself caught within a war between Arab slave traders and African warriors led by Mirambo, who ambushed the Arabs and stormed Tabora but left Stanley and his men alone. The route to Lake Tanganyika was impeded by more fighting, and Stanley was forced to travel south and then north at the Malagarasi River.

In spite of these difficulties, Stanley pushed ahead ruthlessly, exhibiting the characteristics that were to mark all his expeditions. If he encountered opposition, he ordered his men to take out their guns and shoot. If porters shirked their duties, he had them whipped or even hanged. If anyone left the caravan, he had the deserter tracked down, punished, and chained for the rest of the journey. By using harsh methods Stanley met with success. He reached a hill overlooking the town of Ujiji on Lake Tanganyika on November 10, 1871. He had heard reports of an elderly European in Ujiji. Stanley ordered the American flag unfurled at the front of the caravan and marched his column into the town, firing 50 guns simultaneously.

Meets Livingstone

Stanley was met by Susi, one of Livingstone's African supporters, who guided him to where the famous doctor was staying. "As I advanced slowly toward him," Stanley wrote in his book, "I noticed he was pale, looked wearied, had a gray

beard, wore a bluish cap with a faded gold braid round it, had on a red-sleeved waistcoat, and a pair of gray tweed trousers. I would have run to him, only I was a coward in the presence of such a mob—would have embraced him, only, he being an Englishman, I did not know how he would receive me. So I did what cowardice and false pride suggested was the best thing—walked deliberately to him, took off my hat, and said:

'Dr. Livingstone, I presume?'

'Yes,' said he, with a kind smile, lifting his cap slightly.

I replace my hat on my head, and he puts on his cap, and we both grasp hands, and then I say aloud:

'I thank God, Doctor, I have been permitted to see you.'

He answered, 'I feel thankful that I am here to welcome you.'"

Upon meeting the explorer David Livingstone, who had been presumed lost in the African jungle, Stanley gave his now famous greeting, "Dr. Livingstone, I presume?"

Forms friendship with Livingstone

The two men spent the next four months together and developed a close father-and-son relationship. They held in common a Celt heritage, a childhood of poverty, a dislike of British aristocracy, and a short physical stature, which usually led to conflict with taller men. For Stanley the event marked the turning point in his life. They traveled together around Lake Tanganyika and discovered that, contrary to the belief of **Richard Burton** (see entry), the Ruzizi River flowed into and not out of the lake and was not, therefore, the source of the Nile. The two men traveled together back to Tabora, where they stayed for a month, with Stanley trying to convince Livingstone to return to England with him, but Livingstone would not.

On March 14, 1872, Stanley left for England and had fresh porters sent from Zanzibar for Livingstone. Livingstone then headed back to the African interior to investigate the Lualaba River, which was his own favorite candidate to be the Nile source. The Lualaba does flow north from the river flowing out of Lake Tanganyika but is actually a part of the Congo River system. Stanley organized a march column that covered 525 miles in 52 days, reaching Bagamoyo on May 6, a record for miles covered per day in a long-distance march. Bennett cabled Stanley: "You are now as famous as Livingstone, having discovered the discoverer."

Claims are doubted

News of Stanley's discovery, however, was not greeted with the reception he had anticipated. When he arrived in London on August 1, after receiving a hero's reception in Paris, the British aristocracy called him a liar and the Royal Geographical Society doubted his claims. When the Livingstone family confirmed the authenticity of the letters he brought back, he was still looked down upon as a boorish American. However, Queen Victoria received him and the Royal Geographical Society awarded him its gold medal.

When Stanley returned to New York, he received a much better welcome, but some newspapers printed unflattering articles; for example, one mentioned his naval desertion. Stanley

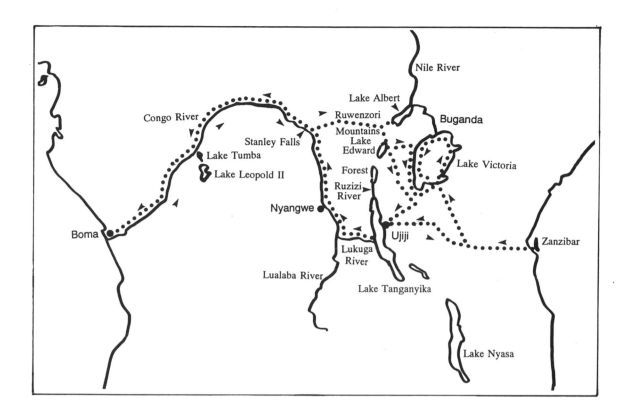

remained bitter about his reception for the rest of his life. His book, *How I Found Livingstone in Central Africa,* was a popular success when published in 1872. His decision to return to Africa was partly an attempt to prove his critics wrong.

Continues Livingstone's work

Livingstone died in Africa on April 27, 1873, and his body was returned to England for burial. Stanley served as one of the pallbearers at his funeral at Westminster Abbey in London. On hearing of his death, Stanley wrote, "May I be selected to succeed him in opening up Africa to the shining light of Christianity!" He then proposed to the London *Daily Telegraph* that it sponsor him on an expedition to Africa in which he would continue Livingstone's explorations. The newspaper agreed, and he left for Africa on August 15, 1874.

The Great Congo Expedition included 356 porters, gun bearers, and camp followers. Stanley had chosen as his com-

Considered one of the greatest African explorers, Stanley made four expeditions to Africa: 1871-72, 1874-77, 1879-83, and 1887-89.

panions Frank and Edward Pocock, two brothers who were fishermen, and Frederick Barker, a London hotel clerk. None of them had been outside England. The expedition's objectives were to sail around Lake Victoria, to explore and map Lake Tanganyika, and to follow the Lualaba River to see where it led. Stanley designed a 40-foot boat he named the *Lady Alice,* which could be taken apart in five sections for portage.

Circumnavigates Lake Victoria

From the beginning, the party experienced difficulties after leaving Bagamoyo on the East African coast. Porters deserted and many people, including Barker and Edward Pocock, suffered from disease. Africans were openly hostile, leading to armed warfare. Stanley persevered, however, and reached Lake Victoria on February 27, 1875. As he sailed around the lake in the *Lady Alice,* he fired at a group of Africans on Bumbire Island with his rifle and shotgun, killing several of them. These and similar actions led to criticism of his methods when he returned to Europe. He did, however, make a complete circumnavigation of the lake and verified the claim of **John Hanning Speke** (see entry) that it was one body of water that drained at the north by the Victoria Nile.

Hostile African tribes blocked Stanley from leaving Lake Victoria and going north to Lake Albert. He had the *Lady Alice* carried over to Lake Tanganyika, and he sailed around the lake, establishing that its only outlet was the Lukuga River on the west shore. He also established that the Lukuga was a tributary of the Lualaba. He traveled down the Lualaba and reached the town of Nyangwe on October 17, 1876, the headquarters of the famous Arab trader Tippu Tib and the farthest point yet reached by European explorers.

Takes perilous trip down river

In return for a substantial payment, Tippu Tib agreed to accompany Stanley with a force of 700 men, and they set off on November 5, 1876. They soon split up, however, with Stanley floating downstream in the *Lady Alice* while Tippu Tib followed on land. The trip lay through a vast tropical rain forest, and the land party suffered numerous casualties from sickness and starvation and frequent attacks by forest tribes. In December, Tippu Tib and his men turned back to Nyangwe, after traveling 125 miles with Stanley. On December 28, 1776, Stanley's party launched 23 canoes and the *Lady Alice* on the Lualaba.

A few miles upstream from the modern city of Kisangani—once known as Stanleyville—they came to the first of a chain of seven cataracts named Stanley Falls. All of the supplies had to be unloaded, the *Lady Alice* disassembled, and everything then carried through the forest jungle and over rocks and cliffs. Soko warriors attacked Stanley on February 1, and on February 14 Bangalas attacked in what Stanley labeled the "fight of fights." Below the falls the river turned to the west, and Stanley surmised correctly that the Lualaba was the upper course of the Congo River.

Travels full length of Congo

On March 12 the party reached a large body of water known as Stanley Pool, which was surrounded with white cliffs; the cities of Kinshasa and Brazzaville now stand there. Below the pool they came to an even wilder series of cataracts that Stanley named Livingstone Falls. At Massassa Rapids, Frank Pocock, the only surviving European besides Stanley, was drowned on June 3, 1877, in an attempt to shoot the rapids. His death deeply depressed Stanley. "I am weary, oh so weary, of this constant tale of woes and death," he wrote.

At the end of July they abandoned the *Lady Alice* and proceeded overland for Boma, a European trading post on the Atlantic coast, sending a message ahead that they were near starvation, and food was sent back. The expedition was reduced to 115 people, including three mothers with newborn children; 277 people had either deserted or died along the way. On August 9, 1877, exactly 999 days after leaving Zanzibar, Stanley led the expedition into Boma. They had traced the entire course of the Congo River, and Stanley's accomplishment placed him equal to **Christopher Columbus** and **James Cook** (see separate entries).

Returns to Congo

Stanley fulfilled his promise to his porters and took them back to Zanzibar in November 1877 before proceeding to England at the end of the year. When he arrived he was condemned in newspapers and Parliament for his ruthless methods. In 1879 Stanley returned to the Congo River on an expedition sponsored by King Leopold II of Belgium to open up economic access to the interior. He spent most of the succeeding years working for Leopold. In 1883 he discovered two major lakes—Tumba and Leopold II—on a tributary of the lower Congo. King Leopold's goal was to have economic control of central Africa and deployed Stanley to set up trading stations. Stanley also subdued the Soko and Bangala tribes of the upper Congo, using a new Krupps gun. To Stanley's displeasure, Arab slave traders used the new passageway of the Lualaba to expand into the upper Congo.

At the Berlin Conference in 1884-85 Leopold maneuvered to gain sole control of the Congo, now called the Congo Free State, which he controlled for the next 23 years. He made a deal with the French that, unknown to Stanley, he would not employ Stanley in Africa. Stanley remained in Europe with no African assignment, but then another grand opportunity for adventure arose. Stanley's reputation, despite his critics, made him the preeminent African explorer of his time, and he seemed the obvious choice to lead the Emin Pasha Relief Expedition.

Leads relief expedition

Emin Pasha was a German who had converted to Islam and worked for the khedive of Egypt as the governor of the Equatoria province in Sudan. When the Sudanese under the Mahdi revolted against Egyptian rule and killed General Charles "Chinese" Gordon, Emin Pasha, Gordon's lieutenant, was cut off from contact with the outside world. Over £20,000 was raised to pay for an expedition to rescue him. British capitalists also envisioned setting up a trading monopoly in East Africa like Leopold's in the Congo.

Leopold agreed to release Stanley from his contract if Stanley would go to Equatoria via the Congo; Leopold also required Stanley to carry the Free State flag on to the Congo. Leopold complicated Stanley's mission. He would now have to cut through the unknown Ituri Forest to reach Emin Pasha, then headquartered on Lake Albert in what is now Uganda, from the west rather than approaching from the more obvious, and much easier, route from the east. Accordingly, Stanley arrived at the mouth of the Congo River on March 18, 1887.

The expedition consisted of 700 Africans hired by Stanley and commanded by eight European officers and 800 Tippu Tib supporters. The expedition was divided into two groups—an advance column and a rear column. Stanley led the advance column up the Congo to its confluence with the Aruwimi River. There Stanley decided to take the advance column with him leaving a rear column behind. In the upper reaches of the Aruwimi they had to fight their way through the Ituri, one of the densest, darkest, and most impenetrable forests on earth. The Ituri is also the home of the Pygmies, who were very adept at maintaining their sanctuary by shooting poison arrows at intruders. The death toll from these attacks and from disease and hunger was high. In one place, 52 men too sick to continue were abandoned to die. The survivors reached the edge of the forest on December 2, 1887, having cut through the 50,000-acre forest. There they waited for Emin Pasha.

Emin Pasha refuses rescue

When Stanley finally met Emin Pasha and his companion Gaetano Casati on April 29, 1888, he was dismayed to discover that they did not feel particularly threatened and did not want to be rescued. The immediate rapport he had had with Livingstone was missing. Emin Pasha thought Stanley had come with guns and ammunition for him, while Stanley believed Emin Pasha was obligated to return with him to the east coast. Stanley argued with Emin Pasha, then returned to his camp. On his way back he saw for the first time a great range of snowcapped mountains in the distance. The clouds on the upper slopes parted long enough to reveal peaks rising to nearly 17,000 feet. This is the Ruwenzori Range, which have been identified with the legendary Mountains of the Moon that the Greek geographer Ptolemy had written of 1,900 years before. They were supposed to be the source of the Nile, and, in fact, some of the water draining from the mountains flows into Lake Edward and Lake Victoria and so to the White Nile.

When Stanley got back to his camp, he found that the rear column had not arrived. He traveled 90 miles into the Ituri Forest before finding the missing men. They had been decimated by dissension and disease, and only 98 out of the original 258 were still alive. He traveled back with them to Emin Pasha's headquarters. By the time they arrived, some of Emin Pasha's troops had rebelled, and there was news that the Mahdists were making gains to the north. In spite of this, Emin Pasha could not make up his mind what he wanted to do. In one final angry confrontation, Stanley disarmed Emin's soldiers and forced Emin to go with him to Zanzibar. Along the way they explored the land south of Lake Albert. They found another large lake that Stanley named Albert Edward Nyanza after Britain's Prince of Wales. It is now called Lake Edward.

Spends last years in England

The party reached Zanzibar in December 1889. Emin Pasha had decided that he did not want to go back and returned to the interior, where he was killed in 1892. Stanley returned to England where he married the artist Dorothy Tennant in 1890. He was naturalized as a British subject in 1892 and served as a Member of Parliament for the London constituency of Lambeth from 1895 to 1900. He died on May 9, 1904. Although knighted, Stanley did not get his wish to be buried next to Livingstone in Westminster Abbey.

Stanley wrote profusely and vividly about his African adventures. Besides *How I Found Livingstone in Central Africa,* he wrote *Through the Dark Continent,* his account of his trip across Africa and down the Congo River. His efforts in support of King Leopold are described in *The Congo and the Founding of Its Free State*. *In Darkest Africa* tells the story of the Emin Pasha Relief Expedition. Following Stanley's death, his wife edited and published his autobiography.

Will Steger

Born 1944,
Richfield, Minnesota

Will Steger is an American who led the first overland expedition to the North Pole since 1909 without being furnished supplies by airplane; he also led an international expedition across Antarctica.

Will Steger is an American adventurer who is fascinated with two of the most inhospitable places on Earth: the North Pole and the South Pole. He led the first overland expedition to have reached the North Pole without air support since 1909; he later headed an international expedition across Antarctica over an 800-mile expanse that had never before been crossed on foot. A self-described former hippie, Steger carries on in the tradition of Arctic explorers such as **Robert Edwin Peary** and **Richard Evelyn Byrd** (see separate entries). However, since Steger is not officially sponsored by the United States, his costly expeditions are funded by numerous television and radio appearances and by private businesses that supply him with goods and services.

Shows early interest in adventure

Steger was born one of eight children in Richfield, Minnesota, near Minneapolis in 1944. From early childhood he was encouraged to explore, experiment, and dream. His interest in exploration was kindled at the age of 12 when he was one of many American schoolchildren who participated in science projects as part of the International Geophysical Year (IGY) in 1957-58. (The IGY was an international program that brought together scientists from 67 nations to study a variety of subjects, including the composition of the sun and the earth, deep-sea currents, and gravity.) Making nightly sky observations, he reported on displays of the northern lights, including one of the biggest recorded in the twentieth century. As part of the IGY activities he also read about the crossing of Antarctica by **Vivian Fuchs** and **Edmund Hillary** (see separate entries), and he decided that he too would someday visit Antarctica.

Steger and one of his brothers were inspired by Mark Twain's *Huckleberry Finn* to float down the Mississippi in an old motor boat. When the boys made it home three weeks later, they had been tossed behind bars for vagrancy and found themselves several hundred dollars in debt. Steger was 15 at the time. When he was 19 he and a school friend made a trip to Alaska and kayaked down the Yukon River. The next summer he kayaked 3,000 miles down the Mackenzie River in Canada to the Arctic Ocean.

After graduating from college Steger taught high school science. In the 1970s he bought a piece of land near Ely in northern Minnesota, where he built a small cabin. He lived there on less than $2,000 a year, growing or hunting most of his own food. He earned his living by leading canoe trips into the wilderness and by teaching winter camping and outdoor skills to tourist groups. In the following years he kayaked more than 10,000 miles, traveled by dogsled another 15,000 miles, and hitchhiked over 100,000 miles. In 1985 he went by dogsled from his cabin in Minnesota to Point Barrow on the northern coast of Alaska.

Leads trip to North Pole

In 1983 Steger began planning a trip over the ice to the North Pole with Paul Schurke, a fellow wilderness instructor.

Steger's aim was to reach the North Pole entirely by dogsled without any resupply by airplanes. This feat had not been accomplished since Robert Peary made the first trip to the Pole in 1909. The Steger International Polar Expedition consisted of seven men and one woman, Ann Bancroft, a schoolteacher from Minnesota. They left from the northern tip of Ellesmere Island in Canada on March 8, 1986.

They had five sleds, each of which carried an initial load of 1,350 pounds. It was impossible for the total of 49 dogs that made up their teams to carry such a heavy weight all at once, so at first they had to travel in relays. They would deliver part of a load to a camp, then go back and get the rest. This was a long, slow process; it took them three weeks to travel the first 80 miles of the 478 miles from Ellesmere Island to the Pole. Along the way as the team members and the dogs consumed the food and fuel they had brought along the load became lighter.

Gradually they cut off parts of the sled and made fires from the leftover wood. This also meant that they needed fewer and fewer dogs to pull the sleds and less food to feed them. On earlier expeditions the dogs had been killed along the way and then either fed to the other dogs or eaten by the humans. For his expedition Steger arranged for planes to pick up the excess dogs at various points along the way; in keeping with his ground rules, however, these planes did not bring in any supplies or give the expedition any navigational or meteorological help.

Encounters difficulties

The expedition suffered various mishaps along the way. The dogs broke out one night and ate a majority of their supplies. One member injured his ribs in an accident with one of the sleds and had to be airlifted out. Another suffered severe frostbite and had to fly back as well. Bancroft fell into a lead, an open stretch of water in the ice, and nearly drowned. Fortunately she suffered no serious injuries and was able to continue, becoming the first woman to travel to the Pole overland. Because the sextant they were using for navigation was slightly damaged, the party went somewhat off course until the discrepancy was spotted.

Achieves goal

During the trip Steger and his team had an interesting encounter. A Frenchman, Jean-Louis Etienne, left from another spot on Ellesmere Island the day after Steger, skiing alone all the way to the Pole. His supplies were air-dropped. Although they were following different routes and were not coordinating their travel, their paths crossed on April 8. While Etienne spent a day in Steger's camp, the two talked of their dreams of crossing Antarctica. After 56 days of grueling travel, Steger and the remaining members of his party reached the North Pole on May 1, 1986. Etienne arrived ten days later. Steger's party was taken off the polar ice by aircraft and flown back to Canada.

Heads expedition to Antarctica

In 1988 Steger began to make the expedition suggested by Etienne a reality. Using a team of experienced international explorers who had never worked together before, he made a south-to-north crossing of the ice cap of Greenland. They tested clothing, dogs, and equipment in anticipation of the Antarctic trip. The experiment was a success, and Steger prepared for his most ambitious expedition with the same team. Their goal was to cross Antarctica at the continent's greatest width.

The team that made up the International Trans-Antarctica Expedition was Steger, Etienne, Victor Boyarsky of the Soviet Union, Qin Dahe of China, Geoff Somers of Great Britain, and Keizo Funatsu of Japan. They left from some rocky outcrops of the Antarctic Peninsula from an Argentine camp called the Seal Nunataks on July 27, 1989. Their route took them across the mountainous Antarctic Peninsula, the first time it had ever been crossed in winter. The day they left the temperature was a warm 28°F, but by the eleventh day it had dropped to zero and they were caught in a storm with winds as high as 75 miles per hour.

The expedition depended for supplies on 12 caches that had been air-dropped along the way the previous year. Because the team was able to find only nine of the caches, there was sometimes a shortage of food for both the men and dogs. During their trip they carried out scientific experiments and observations and took samples of the snow, which gave information about weather history and pollution across the continent. The expedition reached the American Amundsen-Scott Base at the South Pole on December 11, where they were greeted by about 60 people.

Reaches most difficult phase of trip

From the South Pole Steger's expedition entered the "area of inaccessibility," so named because it is equally remote from all coasts of Antarctica. The 800-mile-wide area had never been crossed on foot before. This was the most difficult part of the trip. The explorers had to climb to altitudes up to 11,400 feet where oxygen was thin and they were bombarded with ultraviolet rays. At times solar storms made radio communications almost impossible. It took them a month to cross this region; they reached the Soviet base of Vostok on January 18. They were now in the coldest part of the continent, where temperatures plunged to -54°F, with a wind chill factor of -125°. As they got nearer to the coast temperatures increased, but two days away from their goal of the Soviet base of Mirnyy, they ran into heavy storms.

Braves storms to complete trip

On March 1, 1990, Funatsu left the tent at 4:30 P.M. to feed his dogs and got lost in a blinding snowstorm. At 6:00 P.M. the other team members went out to search for him, but had to give up in a few hours. They started out again at 4:00 the next morning. At 6:00 A.M., Funatsu, who had tunneled into the snow to keep warm, heard their calls. After a dramatic rescue, the weather calmed and all six team members walked into Mirnyy Base on March 3, 1990. They were welcomed by a display of flags of their respective nations and a French television crew that broadcast the event. They missed their target date by only two days. If they had been much later they would have had to stay and endure another treacherous winter. The journey of 3,741 miles had taken 220 days to complete.

Continues to seek adventure

During his career Will Steger has had to use all of his survival skills learned from years of living in wilderness areas. Even though he claims to take only calculated risks, Steger has still had many brushes with death. He says his most frightening experience took place in the lake behind his farm in Minnesota. He was alone when the ice on which he was standing broke. Steger made three futile attempts to pull himself out before he finally scrambled to safety. This close call in his own backyard has made him more determined than ever to live fully for the moment.

Aurel Stein

Born November 26, 1862,
Budapest, Hungary

Died October 26, 1943,
Kabul, Afghanistan

Sir Aurel Stein was a Hungarian who immigrated to England and made several important archaeological expeditions to central Asia.

Sir Aurel Stein spent much of his life investigating the ancient history of central Asia. His greatest find was the "Caves of the Thousand Buddhas" in what was then Chinese Turkestan. A native of Hungary, he became a British citizen in 1904 and was knighted for his work in 1912. Stein's long career did much to enlighten the world about Asia's strategic role in the development of world culture.

Goes to India

Mark Aurel Stein was born in Budapest, Hungary, on November 26, 1862. His well-to-do family sent him to schools in Hungary and Germany, where he received his Ph.D. in archaeology in 1883. He went to Oxford University in England for postgraduate studies in 1884; while he was in England, his parents died. In 1888 he accepted a position at Punjab University in Lahore, India, where he stayed for the next 11 years. During his vacations Stein made archaeological expeditions into Kashmir and the Pamir and Gilgit mountain ranges and published several important works, including a twelfth-century history of India that was written in Sanskrit, the language of ancient India. He accepted another job in Calcutta in 1899, but his great ambition was to investigate the archaeological sites of central Asia. With support from the Indian government, he set out on his first expedition in March 1900.

Leads expeditions to Asia

The goal of Stein's expedition was to explore the ruins of an ancient city in the Takla Makan Desert in western China, which had been discovered by the Swedish explorer **Sven Hedin** (see entry). Stein excavated part of the city, which had perished when its water supply from the Kun Lun Mountains dried up. He also investigated other sites near the city of Khotan, discovering several documents written in ancient languages and a number of artifacts that included neolithic stone tools and textiles. Stein also found ancient caravan routes between China and the West that revealed new information about this little-known region.

Stein's second expedition started in 1906 with a return to the area around Khotan. He went as far as the shifting desert lake of Lop Nor and excavated at Lou-lan, a Chinese outpost from the second century that had also been discovered by Hedin. Stein's greatest discoveries were at Tun-huang where he found the "Caves of the Thousand Buddhas," which contained manuscripts, temple banners, and frescoes. The caves had served as a storehouse from the fifth to the tenth centuries but had been walled off since the 11th century. Stein's discovery is said to be the greatest archaeological find ever made in Asia. Many of the treasures he found are housed in the Asian Antiquities Museum in New Delhi, India.

Appointed head of archaeological survey

In 1907 Stein's expedition explored the Nan Shan range and made a midwinter crossing of the Takla Makan. While exploring the Kun Lun Mountains in the summer of 1908 he suffered frostbite and had to return to India; the toes of one of his feet were amputated. Two years later Stein was appointed head of the Archaeological Survey of India. The organization sponsored him on his longest expedition, which began in 1913. He circled the Takla Makan and explored the Turfan Depression and far northwestern China.

Between 1913 and 1915 Stein made other great discoveries. At Kan-chou he found a hoard of manuscripts in the Tangut and Tibetan languages, and while he was in the region his Indian assistant surveyed the headwaters of the Kan-chou River. In 1915 he found the Sassanian wall paintings in Seistan, having traveled to Persia from Kashgar by way of the Pamir Mountains, Bukhara, and the Amu Darya River. From Seistan the expedition reached the Indus River by crossing Afghanistan. His journey then took him across the Pamirs into Russian Turkestan. Stein returned to India in 1916 by way of Persia and Baluchistan in what is now Pakistan.

Explores Persia

Because of political instability caused by the Russian and Chinese revolutions in the early twentieth century, there was no access to central Asia for several years. In the meantime, Stein made journeys to Baluchistan and Persia. He traced the campaigns of **Alexander the Great** (see entry), providing precise locations of sieges and battles. For instance, in 1926 he identified the place where Alexander led a siege on the Rock of Aronos in present-day Pakistan. From 1927 to 1936 he studied mounds in Iran and Baluchistan, hoping to shed some light on the relationship between the civilizations of Mesopotamia and India.

Stein had wanted to investigate the ancient sites of Afghanistan for years, but political conditions had prevented it. In 1943 he was finally granted permission to travel to the area. A few days after his arrival in Kabul, however, he became ill; he died on October 26, 1943, one month before his eighty-first birthday. During his lifetime Stein wrote several books about his adventures and discoveries.

Abel Tasman

Born 1603,
Groningen, Holland

Died 1659,
Batavia, Indonesia

As a navigator for the Dutch East India Company, Abel Janszoon Tasman made his most famous voyage to the South Pacific, where he became the first European to discover Tasmania, New Zealand, Tonga, and the Fiji Islands. Tasman was born in a small village in the Dutch province of Groningen in 1603. He went to the Dutch East Indies for the first time in 1633, then spent the next ten years sailing the ships of the East India Company on some of the most lucrative trade routes in the world. He traveled from Holland to Batavia, the capital of the East Indies, now known as Djakarta, and called at ports in Taiwan and Formosa in China; he also visited the Philippines, Japan, and Cambodia. Tasman accompanied an expedition searching for islands reputed to be rich in silver and gold along the east coast of Japan.

Abel Tasman was a Dutch navigator who was the first European to visit the islands of Tasmania, New Zealand, Tonga, and Fiji.

Explores Southern Hemisphere

In 1642 Tasman was chosen by the governor of the East

Indies, Anthony van Diemen, to lead a great voyage of exploration into the Southern Hemisphere. His principal task was to determine if the great southern continent, about which explorers had long been speculating, actually existed. Tasman hired as his pilot Frans Jacobszoon Visscher, who had written a book speculating about the location of the continent. Another goal of the expedition was to explore the Indian Ocean in the hope of finding a passage to Chile.

The expedition left Batavia on August 14, 1642, with two ships, the *Heemskerk* and the *Zeehaen*. Tasman led his fleet in a southwest direction to the island of Mauritius in the southern part of the Indian Ocean, which at that time was a base for the Dutch East India Company. When they left Mauritius, they changed direction and sailed due east rather than northeast, which was the well-known route to the East Indies, hoping that they would find the great southern continent.

Discovers Tasmania and New Zealand

The Dutch knew about the northwest coast of Australia because many of their ships had come within sight of land when they were blown off course before turning north to go to Batavia. But they had no idea how far south this land extended. As it turned out, Tasman's course on his expedition was too far south to touch the southern coast of mainland Australia. He sailed until November 24, when he first sighted land: the southern coast of the island of Tasmania, which is off the southernmost tip of Australia. A party of Dutchmen went ashore; although they saw evidence of human inhabitants they did not encounter anyone. Tasman named the island Van Diemen's Land after the Dutch governor; two centuries later the island was renamed for Tasman.

From Tasmania the Dutch ships turned northward as they continued to sail east, crossing the Tasman Sea, which was also named for the explorer. Tasman called the next land he sighted New Zealand after one of the Dutch provinces. It was actually the northern tip of South Island of New Zealand. There Tasman met a Maori tribe, but when the Dutch and Maoris engaged in hostilities Tasman was forced to withdraw.

Searches for passage to Chile

Assisted by Visscher, Tasman continued to search for a passage to the east that would enable them to sail on to the Spanish colony of Chile and open a new market for the Dutch. Although a passage did exist in this area between the North and South Islands, it was nearly impossible to reach because of small islands, heavy currents, and adverse winds. The Dutch were therefore forced to sail north. On January 4, 1643, they reached the northernmost point of New Zealand, which they named Cape Maria van Diemen for the governor's wife.

As Tasman's party continued to sail north they reached the Polynesian islands of Tonga, where the inhabitants proved to be friendly. The Dutch were able to go ashore and get fresh water and food. They stayed about a week, meeting with a chief and trading European metal products for food and curiosities made by the islanders. In February 1643 they sailed west and came upon some of the Fiji islands, but they did not stop.

Tasman's ships met outrigger canoes in Polynesia

Unknowingly sails around Australia

On their return trip Tasman and Visscher chose the same route many later explorers would take: instead of sailing due west, where they would have come upon the eastern shore of Australia, they traveled north and then west along the north coast of New Guinea to the East Indies. They landed at Batavia on June 14, 1643. Tasman never knew it, but he had sailed completely around the continent of Australia. His voyage established that Australia was not attached to any other landmass.

Seeks new passage to Chile

Although Tasman had completed a ten-month voyage during which only one seaman had died, the directors of the East India Company considered the expedition a failure. They had hoped to open a trade route to Chile or at least to find a land that produced valuable products for trade. Persisting in their belief that there was a better route to Chile, they sent Tasman on another voyage. This time the goal was to see whether there was a passage between the coast of New Holland, which is now Australia, and New Guinea that might lead out into the Pacific and on to Chile.

Tasman's party sailed from Batavia in February 1644, traveling along the northwest coast of Australia to Arnhem Land, a large peninsula. Continuing northward, Tasman discovered the Gulf of Carpentaria. Tasman did not find the passage, tho it did exist: it had been discovered in 1605 by the Spaniard Luis Vaez de Torres, who had never publicized his records. Although Tasman did not fulfill his assigned mission he had shown there was a continuous stretch of land between the Gulf of Carpentaria and the Tropic of Capricorn. He was rewarded with the rank of commander and made a member of the Council of Justice in Batavia.

Following this trip Tasman commanded trading ships sailing between Holland and the East Indies. In 1647 he led a trading fleet to Siam, which is now Thailand; he later fought in a war against Spain in the Philippines. He briefly lost his position because of drunkenness but was reinstated. Tasman became a large landowner in Batavia, where he died in 1659.

Annie Royle Taylor

Born 1855,
Cheshire County, England
Died twentieth century,
England

In addition to becoming the first European woman to travel in Tibet, Annie Royle Taylor almost managed to reach Lhasa, the "Forbidden City" and capital of Tibet—a feat that few explorers before her had been able to accomplish. Her difficult and perilous journey is described in her diary, which was published in 1894. Modern readers of Taylor's diary find it strange that she was not interested in the geography and culture of the country she visited. Instead she makes such comments as "Poor things, they know no better; no one has ever told them about Jesus." Yet her attitude was not unusual for Westerners of her time, and her journal is unique because it gives a vivid description of her unusual journey.

Annie Royle Taylor, an English missionary, was the first European woman to travel in Tibet, at a time when the country was forbidden to all Westerners.

Begins mission work as a teenager

Born in Cheshire County, England, Taylor came from a large and prosperous English family. She had a heart condition at birth and as a child she was coddled by her parents and nannies. As the result of a religious conversion at the age of 16 she began to do mission work in the slums of east London. This work caused a rift between Taylor and her family, who were unhappy with the life she had chosen. Although her father begged her to give up her work and "go into Society" like her sisters, she refused. At the age of 28 she made a break with her previous life by selling her jewelry in order to take a medical missionary course.

Goes to China

In 1884 Taylor became a missionary for the China Inland Mission, an evangelical Protestant society founded in 1865. The mission recruited single men and women to carry Christianity into remote areas of China. Taylor was determined to introduce Christianity into Tibet, where Westerners had been forbidden to travel since the journey of the French Catholic missionaries Evariste Regis Huc and Joseph Gabet in 1846.

Taylor worked for seven years on the borders of Tibet, both in Sikkim to the south and in China to the east. Eventually she saw her chance to cross into the forbidden country. In the fall of 1892 Taylor learned that a Chinese Muslim named Noga and his Tibetan wife were traveling to Lhasa, the capital of Tibet. Noga agreed to take Taylor along if she would pay the expenses for all three. Taylor agreed, and the travelers left Tao-chou in the Chinese province of Szechwan on September 2, 1892. Taylor was accompanied by three servants, including a Tibetan named Pontso, whom she had converted to Christianity.

Makes difficult journey in Tibet

Taylor endured an extraordinarily difficult journey into Tibet. Her survival was probably due to her strong faith. No matter what dangers or problems she encountered, she always felt that God would take care of her. "Quite safe here with Jesus" and "He has sent me on this journey, and I am his little woman" were constant notations in her diary. During the trip to Lhasa, one hardship followed another. One of Taylor's servants died along the way and another deserted and returned to China. Taylor and her party were attacked by bandits. They ran out of food. Her horse died from exhaustion as she was riding it, and the yaks they had with them ate the travelers' clothes. Taylor even had to cross rivers ringed with ice by floating on inflated bullock skins. On Christmas Day she boiled a plum pudding she had brought with her from England but was too ill from the altitude sickness to eat it.

Betrayed by servant

Noga turned out to be a treacherous companion. Because Taylor was a Westerner, her entry into Tibet was illegal, and Noga kept threatening to expose her to the authorities. At one point he threw a cooking pot at her and raised his sword to kill her. Fortunately a friendly Tibetan intervened, offering to kill Noga but Taylor would not let him. Noga eventually stole two horses and rode ahead to tell Tibetan officials that he was traveling with an Englishwoman. Taylor and Pontso were left with practically nothing and had to trade their last tent for food. Although they were forced to sleep for 20 nights in the open air in midwinter, they pressed on toward Lhasa.

Arrested and sent home

On January 3, 1893, only three days' travel from the Tibetan capital, Taylor was stopped by Tibetan soldiers. She was put under arrest and placed in a narrow, coffin-shaped hole in the ground. In spite of her pleas, she was told she would have to return to China by the same route she had taken into Tibet. Taylor stood her ground, however, saying she could not make the journey back to China until Noga returned her stolen goods. When Noga was brought to the local magistrate's office he denied all of Taylor's charges. ("I had never heard such lying," she wrote in her diary.)

The magistrate at first ruled in Noga's favor, but Taylor refused to give up. After six days the magistrate provided her with two horses and some money and supplies. Unfortunately, Taylor's trip back to China was even worse than the trip into

Tibet. She and Pontso traveled alone for the 1,300 miles, arriving in Tau-chou seven months and ten days after they had left.

Founds Tibetan mission

Upon returning to the safety of the mission station, Taylor sent the diary describing her journey to mission headquarters in London. It was published in 1894 and brought some fame to Taylor. She left China and went to England to lecture and recruit more missionaries for her Tibetan Pioneer Mission. She set up the headquarters of her mission in the border town of Yatung in Sikkim, which had been opened to trade with Tibet in 1893. Naming her house "Lhasa Villa," she lived there, assisted by two Englishwomen, until sometime between 1907 and 1909, when she returned to England. Nothing is known about the time or circumstances of Taylor's death.

Valentina Tereshkova

Born March 6, 1937,
Maslennikovo, Russia

U ntil she was 25 years old, Valentina Vladimirovna Tereshkova lived quietly as a factory worker and skydiving enthusiast in the Russian city of Yaroslavl. Her life was transformed in 1962, when she entered the Soviet cosmonaut training program and went on to become the first woman to fly in space. From humble beginnings, she was thrust into stardom by a quirk of fate.

Tereshkova was born on March 6, 1937, in Maslennikovo, a village near the Russian city of Yaroslavl. Her father, who was killed in action during World War II, had been a tractor driver on a collective farm in Maslennikovo. After her father's death she moved to Yaroslavl, where her mother found work in a textile factory and where Tereshkova started school in 1945. At age 16 Tereshkova went to work in the Yaroslavl tire factory while continuing her studies at night school. In 1955 she took a job as a loom operator at the Red Canal Cotton Mill and enrolled in correspondence courses at a technical school.

Valentina Tereshkova, a Soviet cosmonaut, was the first woman to fly in space.

Interest in parachuting

At this time Tereshkova became interested in parachuting as a hobby, making her first jump in May 1959 and founding a parachute club at her factory. Although she once landed in the Volga River and nearly drowned, she did not give up and ultimately accomplished 126 successful jumps. She also progressed professionally and politically. By 1961 she was a spinning machinery technician and secretary of the local Communist Youth League. That same year she pursued her fascination with spaceflight, which had begun with the Soviet Union's first successful unmanned space launch, the *Vostok I,* in May 1960.

Tereshkova was so enthusiastic when **Yury Gagarin** (see entry) made the first manned spaceflight in April 1961 that she wrote a letter to the Soviet Space Commission asking to be considered for cosmonaut training. The commission filed her letter along with several thousand others. In early 1962, however, Soviet leader Nikita Khrushchev decided that the country could score a public relations coup against its space rival, the United States, by sending a woman into space. At that time the United States did not accept women for astronaut training and, in fact, would not initiate a program for women for another 20 years. At Khrushchev's urging, the commission reviewed the letters it had received the previous year. On February 16, 1962, Tereshkova and four other Soviet women were chosen for cosmonaut training.

First female cosmonaut

For the first woman in space, Khrushchev wanted to choose an ordinary Russian worker, not one of the many highly skilled Soviet women who worked as scientists or airplane pilots. Tereshkova, with her background as a factory worker and amateur parachutist, was the ideal candidate. When the Soviet Space Commission notified her that she had been selected, she was instructed not to tell her friends or family what she would be doing. Instead, she was to say she had been selected for a women's precision skydiving team. She immediately entered an intensive training program at the Baikonur space center, which involved working in a centrifuge and an isolation chamber, functioning under weightless conditions, and making parachute jumps in a space suit. She also received jet pilot training. Since Tereshkova had no scientific experience, she reportedly had difficulty with space technology, but she applied herself to the course and eventually mastered it.

Tereshkova may not have been the initial choice for the first female cosmonaut. There is some speculation that she was originally selected as the backup pilot to another female cosmonaut who was later disqualified for medical reasons. In any case, Tereshkova was aboard the *Vostok 6* rocket when it was launched shortly after noon on June 16, 1963, as part of a joint spaceflight with the *Vostok 5* rocket. The *Vostok 5,* with Valeri Bykovsky on board, had been launched two days earlier. This was the Soviet Union's second joint spaceflight. In August 1962 cosmonauts Andriyan Nikolayev and Pavel Popovich had flown in two rockets, one trailing the other by a few miles in a single orbit. Bykovsky and Tereshkova, however, were launched into two totally separate orbits that ranged from being only three miles apart to as many as several thousand miles apart.

Bykovsky's and Tereshkova's activities provide insight into early spaceflight. They conversed with one another and relayed television pictures back to Earth. Tereshkova carried out a series of physiological tests as part of a continuing effort to learn about the effects of weightlessness and space travel on humans. When she experienced some seasickness, the European and American press reported she had been violently ill. Actually, she reacted so well that the flight, which had originally been scheduled for one day, was expanded to three days. Tereshkova landed after 2 days, 22 hours, and 50 minutes in space. In order to return to Earth, Tereshkova fired the retro-engine to brake the rocket. As the space capsule reentered the atmosphere, flames caused by atmospheric friction surrounded the capsule, which then stabilized under a small parachute. Tereshkova was ejected through the side hatch and landed in a regular aviation parachute.

Publicity tours and political career
Tereshkova's successful flight made her an immediate celebrity. Upon landing she was whisked to Moscow to deliv-

er an address to an International Women's Peace Congress. She was then scheduled for an exhausting round of personal appearances that required her to travel around the world making speeches on spaceflight and the international role of women. Yet she had time to resume her personal life, renewing her friendship with fellow cosmonaut Andriyan Nikolayev, whom she had met during the training program. They were married on November 3, 1963, in Moscow in a nationally broadcast ceremony presided over by Khrushchev. In June 1964 Tereshkova and Nikolayev had a daughter, whom they named Valentina. Over the years, however, the couple grew apart, and in June 1983 a Soviet news service announced their divorce.

Tereshkova continued her publicity appearances and official functions. She was elected as a member from Yaroslavl to the Supreme Soviet in 1967 and served on the council of the Supreme Soviet from 1966 to 1970 and from 1970 to 1974. In 1974 she was elected to the presidium, or executive committee, of the Supreme Soviet, an important position that she held until 1991.

David Thompson

Born April 30, 1770,
London, England
Died February 10, 1857,
Montreal, Quebec

David Thompson was born on April 30, 1770, in London, England. He attended a charity school that apprenticed him at age 14 to the Hudson's Bay Company, the largest fur-trading company in British North America, now Canada. In September 1784 Thompson arrived at the company's post at Churchill on the coast of Hudson Bay in what is now the province of Manitoba.

Travels in Canada

During his first year with the Hudson's Bay Company Thompson worked for Samuel Hearne, who had been the first European to travel overland to the Arctic Ocean. The next year Thompson was sent to another trading post, York Factory, which was about 150 miles to the south. He made the first of many such trips at the beginning of winter with two local guides. In 1786 he went on a trading expedition to the North Saskatchewan River, and the next year farther west to the

David Thompson, an Englishman who explored much of northwestern Canada, was the first person to travel through the Rocky Mountains to the mouth of the Columbia River.

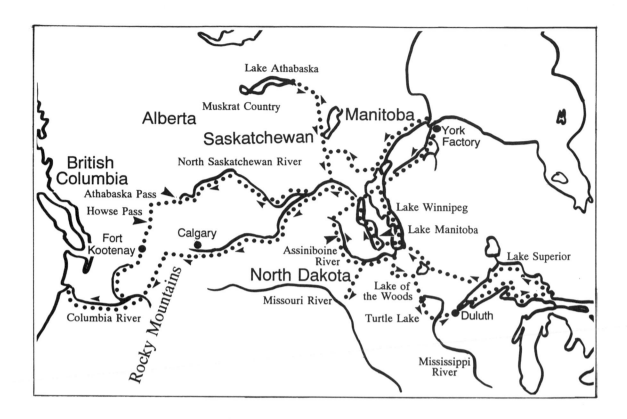

Thompson made numerous expeditions throughout the Canadian northwest to expand the fur trade.

region of the present-day city of Calgary. He spent the winter of 1787-88 with the Piegan Indians and learned their language and customs.

For the next two years Thompson traded for furs in the northern region of the present provinces of Saskatchewan and Manitoba; during his trips he developed his skills in surveying and keeping meteorological records. While returning to York Factory in 1790 he surveyed the 750-mile route.

In 1792 Thompson left York Factory to begin a series of trips into the far north of what is now Saskatchewan. The aim was to find a way to capture the region's valuable fur trade, which was being exploited by the rival Northwest Company, headquartered in Montreal. In 1796 he traveled to Lake Athabaska, the northernmost point of the territory. By this time local affiliates of the Hudson's Bay Company had decided Thompson's surveying expeditions were too time-consuming and ordered him to stop.

Joins Northwest Company

Believing his accomplishments had not received the recognition they deserved, Thompson quit the Hudson's Bay Company, walked to the nearest Northwest Company post, and offered his services to his former employer's competitor. The Northwest Company hired Thompson as a surveyor without any trading duties—he would become a partner. In 1797 Thompson was instructed to survey the new boundary with the United States at 49° N and to travel as far west as the camps of the Mandan Indians along the Missouri River in present-day North Dakota.

During this expedition Thompson journeyed as far as the Assiniboine River before winter. Although he was still a long distance from the Missouri River, he decided to continue, often without a guide. In January 1798 he reached the Missouri River and the Mandan villages, where he stayed until January 10, 1798.

Explores Saskatchewan and Alberta

On the way back he encountered frigid winter weather followed by spring thaws which made travel even more difficult. However, on April 27 Thompson discovered Turtle Lake, one of the headwaters of the Mississippi River in northern Minnesota. He then continued on to Lake Superior by way of the site of modern-day Duluth and surveyed the shores of the lake from there to Grand Portage; he then went northwest to Lake of the Woods, Lake Winnipeg, and Lake Manitoba.

Thompson spent the rest of 1798 and 1799 in the land between North Saskatchewan and Athabaska rivers in what is now Saskatchewan and Alberta. In June 1799 he married a young woman whose father was a Scottish trader and whose mother was Chippewa. After his marriage Thompson always traveled with his wife and numerous children. In 1801 he made an attempt to cross the Rocky Mountains, but could not find a passageway. He then returned to his trading operations in the Muskrat Country. In 1806 the Northwest Company sent him and his family back to the North Saskatchewan River to prepare for another attempt at crossing the mountains.

Discovers Athabaska Pass

In 1807 the Thompson family traveled through the Howse Pass to the Columbia River; Thompson was subsequently credited with being the first explorer to accomplish this feat. For the next three years the Thompsons traveled back and forth across the Rocky Mountains and the Columbia River valley. Thompson founded Fort Kootenay, the first fur-trading post on the Columbia River; he also surveyed the whole area for future traders. Since the Howse Pass had become the battleground for rivalry between the Piegan and Kootenay tribes, Thompson searched for another route across the Rockies. On January 10, 1811, he discovered the Athabaska Pass farther north; it became the usual route across the mountains until the railroad was built years later. In 1811 Thompson traveled all the way down the Columbia to its mouth, but he found that American fur traders sent out by John Jacob Astor had already arrived.

Makes map of western Canada

In 1812 Thompson retired from the Northwest Company and went to live in Montreal. He completed a map of western Canada based on his explorations; from 1818 to 1826 he served as head of the Boundary Commission, which was charged with surveying the border between the United States and Canada. Thompson died in Montreal on February 10, 1857, at the age of 87. He was not recognized as a geographer until after his death, when his maps of North America were used in drawing subsequent maps.

Joseph Thomson

Born February 14, 1858,
Penpont, Scotland
Died August 2, 1895,
London, England

Joseph Thomson grew up reading about the exploits of **David Livingstone** (see entry) and other heroes of African exploration. His work in his father's stone quarry would eventually lead to his own brief but important career as an explorer and adventurer. Thomson became the first European to visit many of the most beautiful and dangerous parts of Africa. The books he wrote as a result of his journeys are valuable for their geographical accuracy and careful detail; his respect for Africans, particularly the Masai, was unusual for that time.

Thomson was born in the small village of Penpont in Scotland on February 14, 1858, in the stone house his father had built. Later his father moved the family to a nearby farm and bought a stone quarry. As a young man, Thomson spent much of his time working in the quarry, an experience that sparked his interest in geology. He wrote several papers on the quarry rocks for a local scientific society. He attended the University of Edinburgh, where he graduated in 1877 with an honors degree in geology and natural science.

Joseph Thomson was a Scottish geologist who made three expeditions to East Africa, during which he became the first European to travel to the land of the Masai in Kenya.

Unexpectedly heads expedition

As a result of his accomplishments, Thomson was chosen to be the geologist on an expedition to East Africa led by Keith Johnston and sponsored by the Royal Geographical Society. Johnston's party arrived in Zanzibar on January 5, 1879. After collecting their supplies and hiring a team of porters, including the experienced caravan leader **James Chuma** (see entry), they departed for the interior in May. Five weeks later Johnston died of malaria, and Thomson suddenly found himself in charge of the expedition.

Although he had no African experience and he was only 21 years old, Thomson decided to accept the challenge. Under the guidance of Chuma, who proved to be an invaluable assistant—in fact, other party members would joke that Thomson was Chuma's "white man"—the party reached the northern end of Lake Nyasa, now Lake Malawi, in September. Thomson became the first European to travel overland to that part of the lake. In spite of being ill with fever, Thomson moved on, arriving at Lake Tanganyika in November. When Thomson reached the Lukuga River on Christmas Day he confirmed that it was the only outlet for the lake. After warring tribes prevented the party from going to the Lualaba River in what is now Zaire, Thomson redirected their route toward present-day Tanzania. Thomson achieved another first by becoming the first European to discover Lake Rukwa. Following the old Arab trade route to Tabora, he led the party back to Zanzibar in July 1880. Only one of the African porters had died along the way; this was an unprecedented record.

Gains fame as explorer

The success of Thomson's first African expedition gave him a considerable reputation. In June 1881 he was hired by the sultan of Zanzibar, who was also the nominal ruler of the mainland, to travel to the Ruvuma River to investigate reports of coal deposits. When Thomson reached the Ruvuma he found that the mineral deposits were shale, which had no commercial value. Taking a roundabout return route to Zanzibar, he reported his findings to the sultan. He went back to Scotland at the end of the year.

Thomson was hired by the Royal Geographical Society to explore the last major portion of tropical Africa. When he arrived in Zanzibar to organize the expedition, he found that Chuma had died; for caravan leader he chose another experienced man, Manua Sera. One of Thomson's goals was to reach to Mount Kenya, which had been sighted from a distance by **Johann Ludwig Krapf** (see entry) in 1849 but had never been visited by a Westerner. However, traveling to Mount Kenya meant penetrating the land of the Masai people, who had a reputation for being warlike and hostile to outsiders.

When Thomson left the coast in March 1883 he took with him a Maltese sailor named James Martin, 130 porters under Manua Sera's command, and a few donkeys. During the first part of the expedition he followed the route of German explorer Gustav Adolf Fischer, who had reached Mount Kilimanjaro the previous year and who had an armed encounter with Masai warriors. Reaching Mount Taveta at the foot of Mount Kilimanjaro on May 5, Thomson climbed nearly 9,000 feet up the mountain.

Enters Masai territory

By this time Thomson was in Masai territory. He had several tense encounters with the Masai but always stood his ground and did not resort to firearms. At one point, he caught their attention by putting some bicarbonate of soda into a glass of water to make it fizzle. As an additional safeguard he joined forces with a Swahili caravan and traveled with it as far as Lake Naivasha, where Fischer had been forced to turn back. In September his party was attacked at Lake Naivasha by members of the Kikuyu tribe; two porters were killed.

Thomson then crossed a 14,000-foot-high range of mountains, which he named after Lord Aberdare, the president of the Royal Geographical Society. He saw Mount Kenya, but the hostility of the Masai forced him to give up his hopes of climbing it. He reached the northcast shore of Lake Victoria on December 10, 1883, but the unfriendliness of the inhabitants forced him to leave three days later.

In Kenya Thomson encountered Masai warriors such as this one, rushing into battle.

Heading back to the coast, he made a detour and became the first European to see the 14,094-foot Mount Elgon, an extinct volcano on the present borders of Uganda and Kenya. He also visited the remarkable prehistoric caves on the mountain's southern slopes. On December 31 Thomson was badly gored by a buffalo; shortly afterward he became seriously ill from dysentery and lay semiconscious for six weeks in a grass hut. Once again his party was being threatened by the Masai so they rejoined the Swahili caravan and resumed their journey. Since Thomson was still quite ill he had to be carried in a litter. In late May, after a journey of 3,000 miles, they reached Rabai, which was inland from Mombasa. Thomson celebrated by getting out of his litter and walking into town.

Honored for achievements

When Thomson returned to London he was well received. He was given a gold medal by the Royal Geographical Society, and his book about his experiences with the Masai was a best-seller. In 1885 Thomson offered to lead the Emin Pasha Relief Expedition, but **Henry Morton Stanley** (see entry) was chosen for the mission. Thomson instead returned to Africa on behalf of the National African Company. This time he went to West Africa to forestall expeditions from the German colony in the Cameroon; the British felt the Germans were attempting to penetrate their territory. Landing on the coast of Nigeria in March 1885, Thomson went up the Niger to the area that is now northeastern Nigeria and carried out successful commercial negotiations with the leaders of the region. He returned to England in September.

By now Thomson's health was seriously impaired, and he spent the following three years recuperating. In 1888 he traveled to Morocco at his own expense and climbed some of the highest peaks in the Atlas Mountains. In 1890 he was hired by Cecil Rhodes's British South African Company to travel to present-day Malawi and Zambia to sign treaties with the chief of the region, placing them under British protection and granting the British mining and trading privileges.

Thomson became gravely ill on this trip and barely survived the voyage back to London in October 1891. Suffering from lung problems, he traveled the following year to Cape Town, South Africa, with the hope that the climate would improve his health. The trip was only briefly beneficial; Thomson died in London on August 2, 1895, at the age of 37. The Thomson's gazelle, an African antelope, was named in his honor.

George Vancouver

*Born June 22, 1757,
Norfolk, England*

*Died May 10, 1798,
Surrey, England*

George Vancouver was a British naval officer who surveyed the Pacific coast of northwestern North America, completing one of the most difficult surveys ever undertaken.

George Vancouver was born the son of a customs official in the town of King's Lynn in Norfolk, England, on June 22, 1757. He entered the Royal Navy at the age of 13 as a "young gentleman" or midshipman candidate. Through family connections he secured an appointment to serve with Captain **James Cook** (see entry) on the *Resolution* during Cook's second voyage to the Pacific from 1772 to 1775. When the *Resolution* approached the continent of Antarctica, Vancouver hung off the front of the ship so that he could truthfully claim to have been farther south than any other person.

Serves in naval battles

Vancouver sailed as midshipman on board the *Discovery* on Cook's third and last voyage, which left England in July 1776 at the time the United States was declaring independence. Vancouver was a party to the events that resulted in Cook's death on February 14, 1779, on the island of Hawaii.

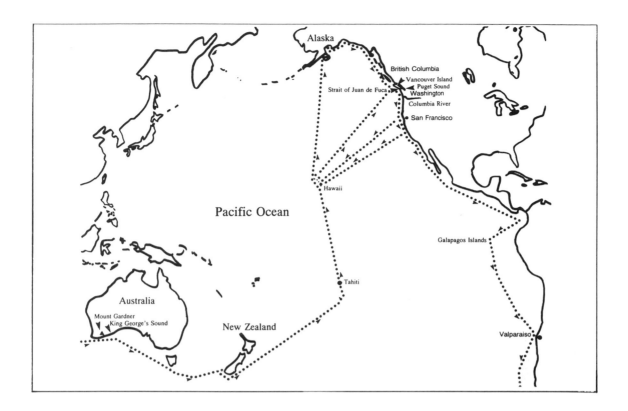

The previous day Vancouver had helped rescue another crew member who had been attacked by a group of Hawaiians, and he was one of the men sent ashore to retrieve Cook's dead body. Vancouver returned to England on the *Discovery* in October 1780; he was immediately promoted to the rank of lieutenant.

During the Napoleonic Wars between Britain and France, Vancouver carried out various assignments in the North Sea and the Caribbean. He fought in a sea battle in the West Indies in April 1782. In 1789 he left active naval duty but was then appointed to be second in command of an expedition to the South Pacific. He took charge of the ship being built for the expedition, which was named the *Discovery*.

Surveys Pacific Coast

At the conclusion of hostilities between Spain and Great Britain, Spain signed the Nootka Convention in which it sur-

During his 1791-95 voyage in search of the western entrance to the Northwest Passage, Vancouver visited several Pacific islands and the northwest coast of North America.

rendered claims to the northwestern coast of North America to the British. Rather than going to the South Pacific, Vancouver was sent to the Pacific Northwest to take formal possession and to make a survey of the coast. On April 1, 1791, he sailed from England in the *Discovery,* accompanied by the *Chatham.*

Vancouver traveled eastward from England, going around the Cape of Good Hope in South Africa and crossing the Indian Ocean to Australia. While exploring along the western coast of Australia he discovered and named King George's Sound, Mount Gardner, and Cape Hood. He then went on to New Zealand and completed information about that coast that Captain Cook had left incomplete. From New Zealand, Vancouver went to Tahiti, which he reached on December 30, 1791.

Sailing north from Tahiti, Vancouver stopped in Hawaii in March 1792. He arrived at a time when a war was going on between the islands, which later led to united rule under King Kamehameha. Vancouver sailed from Hawaii to the coast of California, arriving about 110 miles north of San Francisco Bay on April 18. His instructions indicated that he was to continue the search for the western entrance to a Northwest Passage between the Atlantic and the Pacific.

Claims Pacific Northwest for Britain

As Vancouver made his way north along the west coast of North America, he noted the discharge from a large river off a point that had been named Cape Disappointment. He did not stop to investigate and thereby missed being the first European to see the Columbia River. Two days later Vancouver encountered an American ship, the *Columbia,* whose captain, Robert Gray, reported he had just visited the river and named it for his ship. Gray's statement to Vancouver was later used as justification for American claims to what are now the states of Washington and Oregon.

On May 1, 1792, Vancouver entered the Strait of Juan de Fuca that separates Vancouver Island from the mainland. In the following months he and his men carefully surveyed the coasts of what are now Washington state and British Columbia, including the complex waterways of Puget Sound, named after an officer on his ship, and the Strait of Georgia. He also named Mount Rainier after an officer he had served with in the West Indies. At the end of May, Vancouver claimed formal possession of the Pacific Northwest for Great Britain, naming the country New Georgia in honor of King George III.

Going north through the Strait of Georgia, Vancouver stopped at a bay that he named Burrard Inlet after a fellow officer; it is now the site of the city of Vancouver, British Columbia. On the afternoon of August 6, 1792, near the northern end of Vancouver Island, the *Discovery* ran aground in the fog. Fortunately, it was possible to float the ship out to sea during high tide that night with only minimal damage. The next day the *Discovery* entered Queen Charlotte's Sound, thereby proving Vancouver Island was a separate body of land and becoming the first European ship to negotiate the treacherous waters between the island and the mainland.

Negotiates with Spain

On August 28 Vancouver sailed into Nootka Sound and visited a small Spanish fort commanded by Don Francisco de la Bodega y Quadra. Quadra and Vancouver soon developed friendly relations but came to a stalemate over how Vancouver was to take possession of the Spanish settlement. Vancouver sent a ship back to London to ask for further directions. In the meantime, Quadra suggested that they mark their friendship. Vancouver thereupon proposed naming the large island he had just circumnavigated "Quadra and Vancouver Island." This was the name by which it was known until the mid-nineteenth century, when it was shortened to Vancouver Island. There is now a smaller Quadra Island in the Strait of Georgia.

While waiting for instructions from England, Vancouver continued his explorations. Going south along the coast he stopped at Gray's Harbor, first visited by his American competitor. At the mouth of the Columbia, he sent a party ashore under Captain William Broughton to investigate; they traveled 100 miles upstream to the site of present-day Vancouver, Washington. Broughton also named Mount Hood after a British admiral.

Anchoring in San Francisco Bay on November 14, 1792, Vancouver proceeded to Monterey, the capital of Spanish California, where negotiations continued for the next two months. Vancouver then set out to find the Los Majos Islands that had been reported by earlier Spanish navigators. These early sightings were most likely the Hawaiian Islands. Vancouver landed in February 1793 at the Hawaiian Islands and visited with King Kamehameha, who took him to the site of Cook's murder.

Vancouver returned to America in April 1793. Traveling up the coast of British Columbia, he sailed into Bella Coola inlet just seven weeks before **Alexander Mackenzie** (see entry) arrived at the same spot on July 20 by traveling overland from Canada. The combined results of the Vancouver and Mackenzie expeditions showed the existence of no Northwest Passage around or through North America south of the Arctic.

Surveys Pacific Northwest

During the next several months, Vancouver charted the islands and waters of northern British Columbia, the Inside Passage of Alaska, and the Queen Charlotte Islands. At Revillagigedo Island in southern Alaska, he quarreled with Native Americans, killing as many as ten. He then returned south, stopping at Monterey, where he was not well received by the Spanish viceroy, José de Arrillaga, and going as far as Baja California.

In early January 1794 Vancouver returned to Hawaii. During this visit, on February 25, 1794, he accepted the offer of King Kamehameha to turn his country over to the British, which was never acted upon by the British government. He then headed north and spent the following months charting Cook Inlet, the site of the city of Anchorage, and the southern coast of Alaska. He completed his survey on August 18, 1794. On the way south Vancouver stopped at Nootka and Monterey, where he learned that the Nootka dispute had been settled in the European capitals. He then returned home by way of Valparaiso, Chile, Cape Horn, and St. Helena Island in the South Atlantic. Since France and Britain were at war, he joined a British convoy in the Atlantic; he reached England on October 15, 1795.

Involved in public dispute

In his absence Vancouver had been promoted to captain. Retiring to a village a few miles from London on the Thames River, he used the increase in pay to spend the next few years writing about his voyage. His retirement was marred, however, by a public dispute with one of his former junior officers, Baron Camelford, a relative of British Prime Minister William Pitt. Camelford accused Vancouver of unjustly punishing him during the Pacific voyage and charged him with brutality and tyranny. He challenged Vancouver to a duel, but Vancouver refused to participate. In 1796, when Vancouver encountered Camelford on a London street, the younger man beat him severely with a cane. The results of an investigation of the beating are unknown.

Vancouver had been suffering from a chronic illness, which medical experts think may have been a hyperthyroid condition called Graves' disease, when he died in Surrey on May 10, 1798. He had just corrected the proofs of his three-volume work, *A Voyage of Discovery to the North Pacific Ocean and Round the World*. His brother Peter, assisted by Vancouver's naval lieutenant, Peter Puget, published the book a few months after his death.

Giovanni da Verrazano

Born 1485,
Tuscany, Italy
Died 1528,
Guadeloupe, West Indies

Giovanni da Verrazano, a native of Italy, sailed for the king of France and was the first European to sight New York Harbor, Narragansett Bay, and other places along the eastern coast of North America.

The name Verrazano is familiar to many in North America because of the Verrazano-Narrows Bridge, which spans from Brooklyn to Staten Island, crossing over the entrance ("the Narrows") of New York Harbor. One of the longest suspension bridges in the world, it was named after Giovanni da Verrazano, an Italian explorer, who in 1524 became the first European to sight New York Harbor and many other points along the eastern coast of North America. He also wrote the earliest account of Native American life in that region. Verrazano had been commissioned by the king of France to explore the eastern coast from Florida to Newfoundland with the goal of finding a passage to Asia.

Voyage to North America

Giovanni da Verrazano was born in 1485 into an aristocratic family in the Chianti region of Tuscany, Italy. Pursuing a career as a mariner, he moved in 1506 or 1507 to Dieppe, a port on the northwestern coast of France. From Dieppe he sailed to the eastern Mediterranean and may have traveled to Newfoundland in 1508.

In 1523 a group of Italian merchants in the French cities of Lyons and Rouen convinced the French king, François I, to sponsor Verrazano's voyage to North America. Accompanied by his younger brother Girolamo, who was a mapmaker, Verrazano embarked on the ship *La Dauphine* from Dieppe in early 1524. After crossing the Atlantic Ocean, Verrazano sighted land on March 1, 1524, at or near the site of present-day Cape Fear, North Carolina.

The Verrazano expedition sailed southward for a short distance and then turned back north. The ship landed near what is now Cape Hatteras on the Outer Banks, a sand bar separated from the mainland by Pamlico Sound. Unable to see the mainland from this vantage point, Verrazano assumed that the body of water on the other side of the sandbar was the Pacific Ocean. He concluded that he had found the route to China because Girolamo's maps showed North America as a vast continent tapering to a narrow strip of land near the coast of North Carolina.

Discovery of New York Harbor

Unable to find a passage through what he thought was an isthmus, Verrazano sailed north along the coast, probably stopping at the present site of Kitty Hawk, where he encountered a group of Native Americans. He continued north but missed the entrance to both Chesapeake and Delaware bays. On April 17, however, Verrazano sailed into the upper reaches of New York Harbor, which he described in his journal:

> We found a very pleasant place, situated amongst certain little steep hills; from amidst which hills there ran down into the sea a great stream of water [the Hudson River], which within the mouth was very deep, and from the sea to the mouth of same, with the tide, which we found to rise 8 foot, any great vessel laden may pass up.

He anchored *La Dauphine* at the Narrows, which was later named for him.

Leaving New York Harbor, Verrazano sailed up the coast to the entrance of Narragansett Bay and named one of the islands Rhode Island because it had the shape of Rhodes, the Greek island in the eastern Mediterranean. (More than a hundred years later, Roger Williams would take the name Rhode Island for the new English colony he had founded on the mainland off Narragansett Bay.) Verrazano anchored his ship in present-day Newport Harbor, giving his crew a rest for a couple of weeks. Exploring parties from the ship went as far inland as the site of Pawtucket. From Rhode Island Verrazano sailed up the coast of Maine, proceeding north around Nova Scotia to Newfoundland before returning to Dieppe on July 8, 1524.

Final voyages

Immediately after landing in France, Verrazano wrote a report of his expedition for François I. This report gives the earliest firsthand information about the eastern coast of North America and the Native Americans who lived there. Verrazano's next expedition, in 1527, was sponsored in part by Philippe de Chabot, admiral of France, because King François I was preparing for war in Italy and could not spare any ships. On this trip Verrazano traveled to the coast of Brazil and brought back a valuable cargo of logwood, which is used for making textile dyes.

In 1528 Verrazano undertook another voyage to North America to renew his search for a passage to the Pacific, which he still thought could be found just south of Cape Fear. Leaving France in the spring of 1528, his party apparently reached the West Indies, where it followed the chain of islands northward. After landing at one of the islands, probably Guadeloupe, Verrazano was captured and killed by members of the hostile Carib tribe. His ships then sailed south to Brazil, where they obtained another cargo of logwood and returned to France.

Amerigo Vespucci

Born March 18, 1454,
Florence, Italy
Died February 22, 1512,
Seville, Spain

Amerigo Vespucci was the first to determine that South America was a separate, previously unknown continent that was not a part of Asia. He also worked out a system for calculating exact latitude that enabled him to produce a nearly correct estimate of the circumference of the earth. These two discoveries, which caused a revolution in geography and mapmaking, assured Vespucci a place in history; yet he is perhaps better known as the explorer for whom America was named. Since the time Vespucci claimed to have discovered the continent, scholars have been debating whether he or **Christopher Columbus** (see entry) should be honored for the achievement.

Joins Medici firm

Vespucci was born on March 18, 1454, in Florence, Italy. His studies were supervised by an uncle who instilled in him an interest in astronomy and the study of the universe. In addi-

Amerigo Vespucci was an Italian merchant who led expeditions to the Americas, which were later named in his honor.

tion to being trained in business, Vespucci studied philosophy at the University of Pisa. He served as secretary to his uncle, who was the Florentine ambassador to France, before returning to Florence where he became the manager of a trading firm. The business was owned by the Medici family, the rich and powerful rulers of Florence who had business contacts all over Europe. In 1492 Vespucci was sent to Seville to help with the Medici company, which supplied provisions for Spanish ships sailing out of Seville on their great voyages of discovery. He outfitted the second and third expeditions led by Columbus to the New World.

Takes expedition to New World

Historians are not certain about whether Vespucci went on an expedition to the New World in 1497; however, there is evidence in May 1499 he was able to interest the court in his own expedition to the newfound lands across the Atlantic. He sailed from Cadiz in southern Spain with a fleet of four ships commanded by **Alonso de Ojeda** (see entry), who had sailed with Columbus on his second voyage; Vespucci was the representative of the financial interests backing the current expedition.

When the fleet reached the northern coast of South America after a quick crossing of 24 days, Ojeda and Vespucci went separate ways. Vespucci headed south, becoming the first person to sight the coast of Brazil on June 27, 1499; he was also the first to explore the mouth of the Amazon River. Sailing north to Trinidad, he traveled along the coast of Venezuela to the Spanish colony of Santo Domingo where he replenished his supplies. During the return trip to Cadiz he stopped in the Bahamas and kidnapped 200 Native Americans to take back to Spain as slaves. He arrived in Cadiz in June 1500.

Makes important discoveries

Convinced that there still might be a passage to Asia through the New World, Vespucci sailed again in May 1501, this time in the service of Portugal. During his crossing he met the ships of the Portuguese navigator Pedro Cabral returning from a voyage to Brazil and India. On this second trip Vespucci reached land near the eastern tip of Brazil and entered the harbor of Rio de Janeiro. He is considered the discoverer of the Río de la Plata.

According to Vespucci's account he went as far south as present-day Argentina, a claim that has caused debate among scholars. During his explorations in South America Vespucci developed a system for calculating longitude, which had previously been done simply by dead reckoning, or guesswork. Using this system he correctly estimated the circumference of the earth to within 50 miles of its actual measurement.

Continent named for Vespucci

When Vespucci returned to Lisbon in June 1502 he proclaimed that although his party had not explored the islands off the coast of Asia they had discovered a continent between Europe and Asia that was previously unknown to Europeans. His letter about this discovery, titled *Mundus Novus* (New World), caused a sensation and was translated into Latin, French, Italian, and German.

Vespucci's name was given to North and South America because of an account of his travels, published at St. Dié in Lorraine, France, in 1507, in which he is represented as having discovered and reached the mainland in 1497. It led the geographer Martin Waldseemüller to regard him, rather than Columbus, as the discoverer of the great landmass in the west and to suggest that it be called America in honor of his expeditions.

In 1505 Vespucci was naturalized as a Spanish subject. Three years later he was appointed pilot major of the kingdom, a prestigious position that put him in charge of training and examining pilots and gave him control of the master map. In 1512 Vespucci died of malaria, from which he had suffered during his voyages; he had been planning another trip of exploration to South America.

Vespucci's claims disputed

The question of whether Vespucci made two or four voyages to the New World has long kept scholars occupied. For instance, some historians say he traveled to the continent only twice, in 1499 and 1501, while others believe his accounts of an earlier trip in 1497 and another in 1503. The question of the 1497 voyage is especially important: if Vespucci did discover the new continent before Columbus, he would have had to make that trip, during which he said he reached the mainland. Columbus did not explore the mainland until 1498, when he went ashore on the Paria Peninsula in present-day Venezuela. Some twentieth-century historians tend to believe Vespucci's claims about his discoveries.

Viking

Launched 1975
Decommissioned 1983

The success of the *Mariner 9* mission in orbiting Mars in 1972 led American scientists to conceive of the *Viking* program with the aim of landing a spacecraft on the Red Planet. The mission was named for Scandinavian explorers of the ninth and tenth centuries who discovered North America.

Life possible on Mars

The fourth planet from the Sun with an orbit next in line after Earth, Mars has a period of revolution at 687 days, almost double that of Earth. When the Sun, Earth, and Mars are aligned, the distance of Mars from Earth is 35 million miles; this alignment takes place every 15 to 17 years. When Mars is at its greatest distance from the Sun, it is about 63 million miles from Earth. Scientists believed the dark-colored patches on the planet might be simple forms of life. This could be determined by collecting samples and conducting experiments.

The United States Viking program landed two spacecraft on Mars that conducted experiments to discover signs of planetary life.

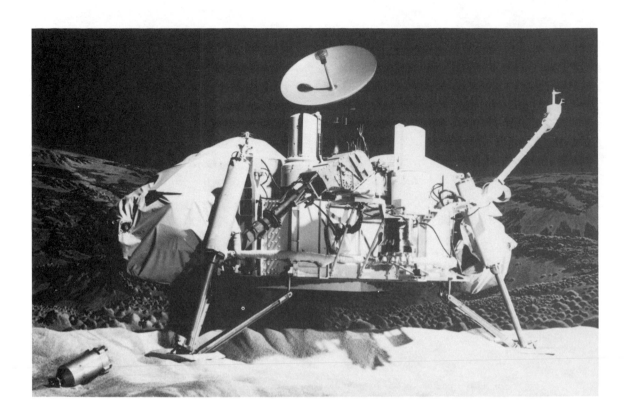

Although designed for six-month missions, the Viking spacecraft operated for a much longer time.

Viking designed to explore Mars

The *Viking* probes were conducted to discover whether life did in fact exist on Mars. The spacecraft consisted of an orbiter–similar to those used in the *Mariner* program–and a lander. The orbiter carried two television cameras and infrared instruments for mapping the planet's thermal characteristics and for detecting atmospheric pressure. The lander, which contained most of the scientific instruments, was a squat, three-legged spacecraft that fit inside a shell for protection while descending through the Martian atmosphere.

The spacecraft would make several orbits of the planet as scientists searched for the least dangerous landing site. Because Mars is strewn with rocks it presented obstacles; for instance, if the lander tipped over it would be useless. Once the lander separated from the orbiter, it would be slowed by both a parachute and a braking rocket. The landing speed was six and one-half miles per hour.

The landers received their power from two radioactive heat sources. Each lander had a robot arm with a scoop at the end that could reach down and pick up soil samples and then drop them into a mini-chemistry lab for analysis. The lander also had a small weather station at the end of a boom and an antenna for communication with Earth. The lander had to be sterilized in hot nitrogen gas to protect Mars from possible contamination by Earth life forms.

First two probes launched

Vikings 1 and *2* were launched on August 20 and September 9, 1975, respectively. *Viking 1* arrived at Mars on July 19, 1976; *Viking 2* followed on August 7, 1976. As part of the celebrations for the bicentennial of the United States, *Viking 1* broadcast a signal to a replica of its arm used to scoop soil samples that then cut the ribbon opening the new National Air and Space Museum in Washington, D.C., on July 1, 1976.

The original landing site was found to be too rough when surveyed by the *Viking 1* orbiter, and another site was selected to the north. On July 20 the lander was set free from the orbiter and descended onto the surface of the Chryse Planitia (Golden Plains). Within minutes it began sending black-and-white photos back to Earth; the transmissions took 18 minutes and 18 seconds to reach Earth. *Viking 2* landed about 3,100 miles farther north on the Utopia Planitia (Plains of Utopia). Scientists were amazed that they were able to land both craft successfully, especially when the first photos showed that the landers had both touched down in the middle of large rocks that could have toppled them or broken their legs. *Viking 1* landed only 26 feet away from a large boulder.

Test soil and atmosphere

The immediate aim of both landers was to search for signs of life. Their scoopers picked up soil samples to be analyzed for signs of carbon-14 and gases given off by live organisms. Two experiments turned out to be especially interesting. In one experiment nutrients that would have supported bacteria were mixed with Martian soil, which decomposed in the way bacteria would have done. In another test air from Earth was released and reacted with the soil the way it would have done in the presence of photosynthesis. However, these experiments were not conclusive and were not matched by others. The scientific consensus was that some kind of inorganic chemistry was imitating organic chemistry. The results were later duplicated by science labs on Earth. The two *Viking* spacecraft found no evidence of life but left open the question if life had once existed on Mars.

The weather stations of the *Viking* landers found results much like those that were expected. Winds were relatively light, reaching about 14 miles per hour. Because Mars is farther from the Sun than the Earth and has a much thinner atmosphere, the planet is much colder. The maximum temperature at the *Viking 1* landing site was -24°F. Temperatures can get as high as 70°F at the equator; since the atmosphere does not retain heat, temperatures descend to -166°F at night. The atmosphere is made up largely of carbon dioxide with traces of nitrogen and argon.

Viking mission a success

Although the two *Viking* spacecraft were designed to operate for six months, they continued for a longer period of time. The two orbiters eventually ran out of thruster gas: Orbiter 2 after two years and Orbiter 1 after four years. Lander 2 suffered a power failure in March 1980, but Lander 1 continued sending back weather reports and photos until March 8, 1983. Plans for a *Viking 3* mission were never carried out.

Viking was one of the most successful United States space programs. A major achievement of the *Viking* mission was an atlas of the planet, *Viking Lander Atlas of Mars,* which was compiled by the United States Office of Space Science and Applications.

Voyager 1 and 2

Launched 1977
Decommissioned 1990

Scale model of a Voyager *spacecraft* ▶

I n 1965 Gary Flandro, an engineer at the Jet Propulsion Laboratory of the National Aeronautics and Space Administration (NASA), discovered a curious planetary alignment through his calculations: the outer planets of the solar system in the late 1970s would be in a rare configuration. The outer planets are Jupiter, Saturn, Uranus, and Neptune–the fifth, sixth, seventh, and eighth planets from the Sun–known collectively as the Jovian planets. The configuration, which happens once every 175 years, would make possible an Earth-launched spacecraft that could fly by the four largest planets. Acting on Flandro's discovery, NASA scientists planned a mission called "Grand Tour."

Spacecraft built

At first scientists proposed construction of four spacecraft, but federal budgetary problems, caused by the cost of building the space shuttle, made only two vehicles possible.

Voyagers 1 and 2 were unmanned American spacecraft that sent back new information about the planets Jupiter, Saturn, Uranus, and Neptune before leaving the solar system for deep space.

Construction of the spacecraft, which were named *Voyagers 1* and *2,* began on July 1, 1972. They each weighed 1,808 pounds and were each equipped with a 12-foot antenna and an onboard computer that could function independently, for years if necessary. Also on board the spacecraft were gold-plated copper records that contained greetings in 60 languages, a series of Earth sounds, selections of music, and 115 pictures, one of which was a map of DNA structure. It would be millions of years before the *Voyager* spacecraft encountered a planet outside the solar system, let alone one with intelligent life.

Spacecraft launched

Voyager 2 was launched on August 20, 1977. *Voyager 1* left Earth on September 6, but because of the route it was following through space it was scheduled to reach Jupiter four months ahead of *Voyager 2.* Some problems were encountered along the way. On *Voyager 1* the scan platform, which turned the cameras and other sensors in various directions, became jammed and would not move until scientists figured out how to fix it. *Voyager 2,* which had a malfunctioning valve that caused a fuel loss until it was repaired, also lost its main radio receiver.

Take photographs of Jupiter

Voyager 1 took its first photographs of Jupiter on December 10, 1978, and then began photographing from distant observations in January 1979 for one month. After crossing the orbit of Sinope, the most distant of Jupiter's moons, on February 10, 1979, it took pictures of two other satellites, Callisto and Ganymede. Pictures of the satellite Io showed geological activity, including one active volcano, Prometheus. *Voyager 1* came closest to Jupiter on March 5, 1979, at a distance of 216,800 miles and traveling 62,000 miles an hour. It photographed the Great Red Spot, a 25,000-mile-wide structure of gas. *Voyager 2* reached its closest approach to Jupiter on July 9. It took photos of Ganymede and Europa and then was reprogrammed to move closer to Io, which turned out to be the most fascinating of the Jovian moons. The two spacecraft took a total of 31,000 photographs. They also confirmed the existence of rings around Jupiter similar to Saturn's but invisible from Earth.

Voyagers reach Saturn

Voyager 1 reached Saturn in November 1980, followed by *Voyager 2* nearly a year later, in August 1981. Saturn is almost twice as far from Earth as Jupiter and receives about 1 percent of the solar energy that hits Earth. Making its closest approach on November 12, *Voyager 1* found spokes coming out of the planet's B ring and discovered three new satellites. Both spacecraft took numerous pictures of Saturn's rings, which sometimes appeared braided or wavy, in defiance of the known laws of physics.

The spacecraft also were able to penetrate the atmosphere of the moon Titan, which is covered with a mixture of nitrogen and methane thought to be similar to the early atmosphere of Earth. Saturn's moons Enceladus, Dione, and Rhea all showed signs of volcanic activity, and Mimas had an impact crater that had displaced an area one-third of its size. The *Voyager* flights also confirmed that Saturn gave off more heat than it absorbed, showing that it may have been a "failed" star.

Complete tour planned

At the time of launching the two *Voyager* spacecraft, the plan was to send them only to Jupiter and Saturn because a complete "Grand Tour" of the planets was thought to be too expensive. However, the spectacular success of the project convinced the scientists that a complete tour was a one-time opportunity. A new route was plotted for *Voyager 1* while *Voyager 2* was aimed at Uranus and Neptune. *Voyager 2* was almost scrapped in a budget-cutting measure in 1980, but was salvaged at the last minute and reprogrammed for a Uranus rendezvous. Five days before the craft's closest approach, a piece of binary code in the processor switched from "0" to "1." An all-night effort was made to route data around the error. It worked.

Voyager 2 makes more discoveries

The closest approach to Uranus came on January 24, 1986. *Voyager 2* took incredible close-up pictures of the planet, which is on a different axis from all the other planets in the solar system because the poles are on the equator and the planet's rings circulate north to south. *Voyager 2* took pictures of the five known moons of Uranus–Titania, Ariel, Umbriel, Oberon, and Miranda–and discovered ten new ones. Miranda, a small satellite nearest Uranus, was found to be one of the most bizarre features in the solar system, with characteristics like Mercury and Mars as well as some of the moons of Jupiter and Saturn. *Voyager 2* photographed the nine known rings of Uranus and found two new ones.

Voyager 2 reached its closest approach to Neptune, 3,048 miles, on August 25, 1989. Neptune is three billion miles from the Sun. It was discovered by mathematical deduction in 1846 and has not yet made a complete 165-year trip around the Sun since its discovery. At the time of *Voyager 2*'s visit, it was the farthest known object in the solar system; the small planet Pluto has an orbit that sometimes brings it closer to the Sun. *Voyager 2* discovered six moons around Neptune in addition to the two known ones and found Neptune to be a large mass of violent, swirling storms with an atmosphere of high white clouds, which are probably methane. The planet also contains a Great Dark Spot, or a great storm of gases, on its surface.

A set of at least four rings was also discovered around Neptune. Some of the rings appear to have arcs consisting of a higher density of material than at other parts of the ring. Pictures of the satellite *Triton* showed it to be slightly smaller than Earth's moon, with two great color bands of salmon and blue. It is one of the brightest and coldest points in the solar system, and its peculiar orbit indicated that it had been captured by Neptune fairly recently.

Voyagers send final pictures

On August 29, 1989, *Voyager 2,* the first man-made object to be sent out into the universe, was 2,758,530,928 miles from Earth and was leaving the solar system. At that time its cameras were turned off to save energy, but it will continue sending data about interstellar space back to Earth for years to come. On February 14, 1990, *Voyager 1,* still climbing after having been separated from *Voyager 2* at Saturn, sent back one last photo, a snapshot taken 3.7 billion miles from Earth showing all of the planets except Pluto lined up in their orbits.

Charles Wilkes

Born 1798,
New York, New York

Died 1877,
Washington, D.C.

Charles Wilkes, who led an important American scientific expedition to the Pacific, was one of the discoverers of the continent of Antarctica.

Charles Wilkes was born in New York City, the son of a prosperous businessman. After being educated by his father in mathematics and navigation, he joined the merchant marine in 1815; he was appointed a midshipman in 1818. Wilkes continued his studies of navigation and astronomy and in 1833 was appointed head of the Navy's Depot of Charts and Instruments, which later became the Naval Observatory and the Hydrographic Office.

Heads expedition to study oceans

For many years the U.S. government had discussed the idea of sending an exploring expedition to make a scientific study of the world's oceans. On May 14, 1836, President Andrew Jackson signed a bill that created the U.S. South Seas Surveying and Exploring Expedition. In 1838, after many false starts, Wilkes was appointed to head the expedition although he was only a lieutenant.

Wilkes departed from Norfolk, Virginia, in August 1838 in the flagship *Vincennes,* which was accompanied by five other aged and not very seaworthy ships. The expedition included naval officers charged with studying the oceans and several civilian scientists who were to study the natural history of the lands they visited. Since the exploring party spent most of the first year at sea, the scientists had little opportunity to carry out their work.

In January 1839 Wilkes's squadron sailed around Cape Horn at the tip of South America and entered the oceans near Antarctica for the first time. Sailing among the Pacific islands, they surveyed a total of 280 islands until they reached Sydney, Australia, in November 1839. Leaving the natural scientists in Sydney, Wilkes went south to visit Antarctica in December.

Explores Antarctic mainland

On January 16, 1840, Wilkes was able to navigate through the ice that surrounded the continent of Antarctica. At a distance he saw an island lying off the mainland; three days later he sailed into a deep bay and definitely sighted land. Coincidentally, this was the same day the French explorer **Jules-Sébastien-César Dumont D'Urville** also saw the mainland of Antarctica for the first time. These were the first two confirmed sightings of the mainland of Antarctica. Unconfirmed sightings had previously been made by **Fabian Gottlieb von Bellingshausen** (see separate entries) in 1820 and by American and British whaling captains in 1829; the English sealing captain John Biscoe had landed on and named Adelaide Island off the Antarctic Peninsula in 1832.

Two weeks later Wilkes was able to sail the *Vincennes* through a maze of icebergs into a bay along the mainland and approach within a half-mile of the coast. He named the place Piner's Bay after a member of his crew; this portion of the Antarctic coast is known as Wilkes Land. Although his crew was by now near mutiny and wanted to turn back to Sydney, Wilkes pressed on as far as 100° E and discovered the area that is known as the Knox Coast. In February, when the ship was stopped by a large ice barrier that was later named the Shackleton Ice Shelf, Wilkes sailed north toward the Pacific Islands and Hawaii.

Explores Hawaii and Pacific Northwest

Along the way Wilkes explored Fiji Island and then led the expedition to the Hawaiian islands; while they were in Hawaii one of the scientists set up an observatory on the volcanic peak of Mauna Loa. In May 1841 the party entered the Strait of Juan de Fuca on the Pacific coast of the United States, then explored the Pacific Northwest; altogether they charted 800 miles of streams and coasts. They returned to Hampton Roads, Virginia, in July 1842, having sailed more than 80,000 miles (completely around the world) and collecting materials for a number of scientific fields, including zoology, botany, anthropology, geology, meteorology, and hydrography.

Writes reports of expedition

Soon after his return Wilkes was court-martialed for mistreating his crew, but he was eventually cleared of most of the charges. He was promoted to the rank of commander in 1843. During the years between 1844 and 1874 Wilkes worked on the reports of the expedition: his five-volume *Narrative of the United States Exploring Expedition* was published in 1844, and he edited the 20 scientific reports, writing two of them himself. Congress authorized the publication of these works, but budgeted only enough money to print 100 copies.

Causes international incident

During the U.S. Civil War Wilkes had a checkered career. When the war broke out he was commander of the *San Jacinto,* a ship designed to keep Confederate traders from reaching port. On November 8, 1861, he stopped the British mail ship the *Trent* and removed two Confederate representatives, James Mason and John Slidell, who were on their way to Europe. Although this action, which is known as the Trent Affair, made Wilkes a hero in the United States, it caused an international incident. The two men were released and President Abraham Lincoln condemned Wilkes's behavior in order to avoid a war with Britain.

In September 1862 Wilkes was commissioned as a commodore and put in charge of U.S. operations in the Caribbean. Although he failed to capture any Confederate ships he offended several foreign governments, which complained of neutrality violations. Wilkes was recalled and demoted; in 1864 he was court-martialed for insubordination and suspended from duty. Later commissioned as a rear admiral, he retired in 1866; he lived in Washington until his death in 1877.

Hubert Wilkins

Born October 31, 1888,
Mount Bryan East, Australia

Died December 1, 1958,
Framingham, Massachusetts

Sir Hubert Wilkins was an Australian-born British explorer who pioneered flying in both the Arctic and Antarctic.

Sir George Hubert Wilkins led a colorful life. He immersed himself in a variety of occupations that offered adventure and challenge, but he is best remembered for his exploration of the Arctic and Antarctic. Wilkins was born on October 31, 1888, in the Australian outback on a sheep station about 100 miles north of the city of Adelaide. At 20 he left Australia by hiding on a ship headed to Algiers in North Africa. He worked as a smuggler until he reached England, where he became one of the first film photographers. He learned how to fly in 1910 and then was sent by his employers to film the Balkan Wars for newsreel services.

Has numerous adventures

Within a period of 12 years Wilkins pursued three different occupations and had numerous, sometimes life-threatening, adventures. In 1913 the *Times* of London hired him as a photographer to cover the Canadian Arctic Expedition led by

Vilhjalmur Stefansson. Wilkins spent two years in the Arctic, at one point saving Stefansson's life when the explorer got lost. After returning to Europe in 1915 Wilkins photographed battles on the Western Front during World War I; he was gassed, wounded nine times, and buried by bomb blasts on several occasions. Following the war he served as the navigator for an airplane crew that was attempting to be the first to fly from England to Australia. Engine failure caused the plane to crash into a mental institution on the island of Crete in the Mediterranean.

Then in a complete change of pace, Wilkins was chosen to be the naturalist on an expedition led by **Ernest Shackleton** (see entry) to Antarctica in 1920. After Shackleton died of a massive heart attack during the trip the party tried to carry on but soon became stuck in the ice; however, Wilkins's work in collecting specimens was favorably noted. He then returned to Europe to make a documentary about the famine in Russia caused by the Russian Revolution. From 1923 to 1925 the British Museum hired Wilkins to lead an expedition to Northern Australia to study mammals and to film the life of the Aborigines.

Leads Arctic expedition

In 1926 Wilkins was chosen to lead the Detroit Arctic Expedition, sponsored by American automobile manufacturers, to the Arctic Ocean in two airplanes to search for new land, including the reported but nonexistent Keenan Land. The expedition traveled from Seattle, Washington, to Fairbanks, Alaska, where both planes crashed. The planes were damaged only slightly and there were no human injuries; however, a reporter was killed when he walked into a propeller. After Wilkins repaired one of the aircraft he flew 150 miles north across the Arctic Ocean to Point Barrow, Alaska. He made several flights to and from Point Barrow but repeated mechanical problems thwarted his progress.

When Wilkins returned to Alaska in February 1927 with a new airplane, he flew 500 miles over the Arctic Ocean. Yet like his previous trip, this one was beset with mechanical problems. During one flight a malfunctioning engine forced Wilkins and his pilot, Carl Eielson, to land on an ice floe. Taking advantage of the situation, Wilkins took depth soundings that showed the ocean to be about 16,000 feet deep at that point, much deeper than anyone had thought. After he and Eielson had repaired the plane's engine they had to land almost immediately because there were still mechanical problems. At sunset they tried to take off again, but as soon as the plane was airborne they ran into a snowstorm. Then they ran out of fuel and were forced to land in a snowbank on an ice floe 65 miles northwest of Point Barrow. Wilkins and Eielson walked overland for 13 days to Point Barrow. More than once during the trip they fell into the water; on one occasion Wilkins, who could not swim, was almost carried away by the current—only an air pocket in his backpack saved him from drowning.

Sets Arctic record

In 1928 Wilkins and Eielson returned to Point Barrow in a Lockheed Vega; they intended to fly across the Arctic from Alaska along the northern edge of the Canadian Arctic islands and Greenland to Spitsbergen off the northern end of Scandinavia. They left Point Barrow on April 5, 1928, following their flight plan until they ran into a storm near Spitsbergen. They flew over a small, isolated island but could find no place to land. After several other attempts, they finally landed in a snowbank on the island.

They remained there for four days until the storm broke. When they tried to leave, they found the skis at the bottom of the plane frozen so solidly that Wilkins had to stay on the ground and push while Eielson flew the plane. After Eielson was airborne he threw a rope to Wilkins, who tried to catch it in his mouth. Not only were all of Wilkins's teeth loosened, but he was also hit by the plane's tail and knocked into the snow. Eielson's third rescue attempt was successful and the two men were finally able to land at Green Harbor in Spitsbergen.

Wilkins and Eielson had made the first flight in a heavier-than-air craft across the Arctic; in 1926 Norwegian explorer **Roald Amundsen** (see entry) and Umberto Nobile had flown across the North Pole in the dirigible, or rigid airship, the *Norge*. After Wilkins's flight Amundsen said, "No flight has been made anywhere, at any time, which could be compared with this." The British government knighted Wilkins; the Royal Geographical Society also awarded him a medal.

Makes first Antarctica flight

Following this accomplishment, Wilkins became the first person to fly an airplane in Antarctica. He and Eielson headed south at the end of 1928 on an expedition sponsored by the Hearst newspapers and named the Wilkins-Hearst Expedition. Wilkins and Eielson made their first take-off on November 16, 1928; four days later, they flew 600 miles over the continent from their base on Deception Island. Wilkins did not try to fly over the South Pole, a feat that **Richard Evelyn Byrd** (see entry) accomplished about a week later. Weather conditions did not permit Wilkins to continue flying. He returned in December 1929 and made a limited number of flights over the Graham Peninsula and west of Peter I Island, but was again forestalled by bad weather.

Attempts submarine trip

On his return from Antarctica in 1930, Wilkins was able to convince the American explorer **Lincoln Ellsworth** (see entry) to help subsidize his next adventure–sailing a submarine under the ice at the North Pole. Wilkins purchased a surplus World War I submarine from the U.S. Navy, which he had refitted and named the *Nautilus*. The ship sailed for Spitsbergen on August 18, 1931, for a trial run under the ice. The submarine had mechanical problems and the crew, apprehensive about sailing under the ice, went so far as to sabotage the *Nautilus*. The attempt was finally abandoned on September 8, 1931, after the submarine sailed a few hours under the ice. It was some 25 years later before a second submarine, again named the *Nautilus,* accomplished the feat envisaged by Wilkins.

Claims territory for Australia

In the following years Wilkins went to Antarctica twice with Ellsworth. Then in the winter of 1937-38 he organized a four-month effort to find a Russian pilot lost over the Arctic. These flights furnished valuable information on the climate and ice movements of the Arctic Ocean north of Siberia. At the end of 1938, Wilkins went back to Antarctica on an expedition sponsored by Ellsworth; in January 1939 he set off on his own to put out markers claiming the area of the Vestfold Hills as Australian territory.

Works for the United States

During World War II Wilkins worked for the U.S. government in supplying aircraft for the war effort. In the early part of the war, he was aboard two different aircraft that were shot down, one over France and one over the Mediterranean, but he escaped unharmed both times. After the war he became an adviser to the U.S. military on Arctic warfare and on camouflage. He died of a heart attack in a hotel in Framingham, Massachusetts, on November 30, 1958. In response to a request he had made several times, his ashes were scattered near the North Pole in March 1959, when the U.S. submarine *Skate* surfaced in the Arctic Ocean. Wilkins wrote about his experiences in his book *Flying the Arctic*.

Fanny Bullock Workman

Born January 8, 1859,
Worcester, Massachusetts

Died January 22, 1925,
Cannes, France

F anny Bullock was born in Worcester, Massachusetts, on January 8, 1859. Her mother was the daughter of a wealthy Connecticut businessman, and her father was a politician who was elected governor of Massachusetts in 1866. In 1881 Fanny married Dr. William Hunter Workman, who was 12 years her senior. They had one daughter, who spent most of her years in boarding schools while her parents traveled.

Bike trips through Europe and Africa

In 1889 Dr. Workman gave up his practice in Worcester because of ill health. The Workmans moved to Germany, which they used as their base for making a series of travels by bicycle throughout Europe. In 1895 they took a long cycling trip to Spain and then to Morocco, where they crossed the Atlas Mountains into the Sahara Desert in Algeria.

On their journey they carried just 12 to 20 pounds of luggage, though Fanny herself was burdened by her typical riding

Fanny Bullock Workman was an American who traveled with her husband by bicycle in North Africa and Asia in the early 1900s. She then became a mountain climber and set two altitude records for women.

outfit, a long, Victorian-style dress. Averaging 50 miles a day, the Workmans stopped to eat and sleep at inns along their route. They were often nearly run off the road by mule trains and got into several arguments with mule drivers. The couple wrote about their adventures in two books, *Algerian Memories* (1895) and *Sketches Awheel* (1897).

Cycling in India and southern Asia

Pleased with the success of their North African trip, the Workmans next tackled a more difficult terrain–India. They traveled, always on bicycle, from the extreme south of India into Kashmir in the north, then from the east coast to the west, and into Burma, Sri Lanka, Java, and Indochina. They kept rigidly to a schedule during all of their travels; when some of their photographs were lost in a flood in Kashmir, they revisited the spots they had seen in order to take the same photos over again. They spent three years covering the length and breadth of India and southern Asia.

Fanny sets climbing records

While in Kashmir, the Workmans had taken time to climb some of the mountains in the Karakoram Range. In 1899 Fanny set a world altitude record for women by climbing Mount Koser Gunge to a height of 21,000 feet. This first experience of climbing thrilled the Workmans, and they then became serious mountain climbers, making eight expeditions to the Himalayas from 1898 to 1912. In 1906 Fanny set a new world record by climbing Pinnacle Peak in the Nun Kun Range to an altitude of 22,815 feet.

In 1908 **Annie Smith Peck** (see entry), the American mountain climber, claimed to have bettered that record by climbing a higher peak in the Andes. Upon hearing the news Fanny hired scientists to measure the peak and proved that it was not quite as tall as the one she had climbed. The Workmans used their expeditions to map and measure the Himalayan terrain. They were not deterred from their goal even when one of their porters was killed when he fell into an icy crevasse. In an amusing tribute to Fanny's status as an independent woman, a photo shows her atop a peak in the Karakoram mountains reading a paper titled "Votes for Women."

Fanny becomes noted woman

The Workmans' travels made them famous. Fanny became the second woman–**Isabella Bird** (see entry) was the first–to address the Royal Geographical Society; she was the first American woman to lecture at the Sorbonne in Paris. During World War I, the Workmans lived at Cannes in the south of France. Fanny died in Cannes on January 22, 1925, after being ill for many years. Her husband took her ashes back to Worcester, Massachusetts, where he stayed until 1937. A memorial to the Workmans was later erected in Worcester; it reads, "Pioneer Himalayan Explorers."

Saint Francis Xavier

*Born April 7, 1506,
Sangüesa, Spain*

*Died December 3, 1552,
Shang-ch´uan, China*

*One of the first
Europeans to travel in
Japan, Saint Francis
Xavier was a Roman
Catholic missionary.*

Francis Xavier was born in his family's castle of Xavier near the town of Sangüesa in the Basque country of northern Spain on April 7, 1506. His father, Juan de Jasso, was the president of the council in the court of the king of Navarre. Xavier grew up in Navarre, where he also received his early education. In 1525 he went to study at the University of Paris; he graduated with a master of arts degree in 1530, then lectured at one of the colleges of the university. While at the university Francis Xavier became an associate of Ignatius Loyola, the founder of the Society of Jesus, or the Jesuits. Xavier took the vows of poverty and chastity in August 1534; he studied theology until 1536 when he went to Venice, Italy, to be ordained as a priest on June 24, 1537.

Sent to Portugal and India

Xavier was sent to Lisbon in 1540 by the pope with a recommendation to King João III of Portugal that he be assigned as a missionary to the Far East, where Portugal was the leading European trading nation. He left Portugal on April 7, 1541, spent the following winter in the Portuguese province of Mozambique, and arrived at the Portuguese city of Goa in India on May 6, 1542. He made a trip to Travancore in southern India in 1543 and is credited with baptizing 10,000 Indians into Christianity while there. On his return to Goa he was appointed chief of all Catholic missions east of the Cape of Good Hope in southern Africa.

In 1545 Xavier traveled to Portuguese posts in southern India and then went to the great trading center of Malacca in what is now Malaysia. In 1546 he traveled to the Moluccas, or Spice Islands, in eastern Indonesia. He returned to Malacca in July 1547. In Malacca he heard for the first time about the distant islands of Japan, where three Portuguese traders had landed in 1542 after having been shipwrecked while on a voyage to northern China. As news of Japan filtered back to the Portuguese trading stations, Xavier determined to go to the country himself. First, however, he returned to India.

Brings Christianity to Japan

Xavier left Goa bound for Japan on April 15, 1549, with two Jesuit companions and three young Japanese who had come with a Portuguese trader to Malacca and had been converted to Christianity. They arrived at the port of Kagoshima on the southern Japanese island of Kyushu on August 15, 1549. Xavier stayed in Japan for two years. During that time he traveled to the port of Hirado on a small island off the west coast of Kyushu.

Xavier then traveled to the castle town of Yamaguchi, which was the headquarters of the Ouchi clan, the feudal rulers of western Japan. At Yamaguchi he argued matters of theology with Buddhist monks of the Lotus and Zen sects. When he visited the capital of the emperor of Japan at Kyoto, he found the city in political turmoil, so he returned to Yamaguchi. At Bungo, the center of the Otomo clan, he was warmly accepted; the head of the Otomo clan converted to Christianity and welcomed Xavier's successors.

As a result of Xavier's visit, a Roman Catholic mission was founded on the southern island of Kyushu and had a great deal of success over the following decades. By the year 1615 there were an estimated 500,000 Christians in Japan. At that time, however, the Tokugawa military governor had started to persecute Christians and to cut Japan's ties with the rest of the world. The Portuguese were expelled in 1639, and contact with Europe was limited to a small Dutch trading post in the southern city of Nagasaki, which had been founded by Christians in the 1560s and was sometimes ruled by Jesuits.

Decides to visit China

Xavier left Bungo in November 1551, reaching Goa in the middle of February 1552. He had decided his next goal was to start missions in China. However, the great Chinese empire, becoming wary of foreign influence and power, was zealously guarding entry into its domains. A Portuguese ambassador was sent out to try to get permission for Xavier to travel to China and to secure the release of some Portuguese who were being held in Canton. The Chinese refused even to talk to the ambassador. Having left Goa on April 17, 1552, Xavier was already in Malacca and he decided to enter China on his own, without official permission. At the end of August Xavier reached the small island of Shang-ch'uan in the Pearl River estuary near Canton, where the Portuguese had been allowed to set up a small trade fair. He became ill in November and died at Shang-ch'uan on December 3, 1552. He was made a saint of the Roman Catholic church in 1622.

Xenophon

Born c. 431 B.C.,
Athens, Greece

Died c. 352 B.C.,
Corinth, Greece

X enophon led a Greek army on a harrowing retreat across Asia Minor, then wrote a vivid account of the event that is still being published and read today, almost 2,400 years later. Exiled from his native city of Athens for most of his life, Xenophon wrote prolifically on a variety of subjects. He is the most celebrated of the early Greek historians.

Born in the Greek city-state of Athens, Xenophon became a pupil and companion of the famous Greek philosopher Socrates. He was also trained in horsemanship, which may indicate that his father held considerable wealth and probably land. Following the death of King Darius II of Persia, Xenophon became involved in the struggle of Darius's two sons over the succession to the Persian empire. The elder son, Artaxerxes, became king, but the younger son, called Cyrus the Younger, coveted the crown for himself. In 401 B.C. Cyrus attempted to overthrow his brother with the aid of a Greek mercenary army, known as the Ten Thousand. Xenophon was one of the soldiers who joined this force. Twenty years after

Xenophon was a Greek soldier who led an army across Asia Minor in an epic march that he later described in a famous travel book.

the event he wrote an account of the campaign in the *Anabasis,* which means "March into the Interior."

Describes retreat through Persia

Xenophon tells how the Ten Thousand, led by Cyrus, marched into Persia and waged a great battle at Cunaxa, 45 miles from Babylon, in what is now Iraq. Cyrus was defeated and killed; 24 Greek generals were captured and put to death. Stranded in a foreign and hostile land without any leadership, the Greek soldiers elected their own generals. Xenophon was chosen to be second-in-command to the Spartan Cheirosophus.

Xenophon became the inspiring force for this refugee army on its torturous 1,500-mile trek back to Athens. Marching out of Persia, they were harassed by the Persian army, under the command of Tissaphernes, until they reached the mountains of Kurdistan. Then the Greeks had to fight against fierce Kurdish tribes through the mountains to the border of the Kingdom of Armenia at the Centrites River, a tributary of the Tigris, in eastern Turkey. In Armenia they were met by a force led by Tiribazus, the ruler of Armenia. In order to secure their safe passage, the Greeks had to promise Tiribazus that they would not live off of his land during their journey.

Leads mountain crossing

By now it was December, and the highlands of Armenia were covered with ice and snow. The Greeks had to follow a route through territory so rugged that it was little known until modern times. To make matters worse, because of their promise to Tiribazus, they had only meager resources. They suffered greatly from frostbite and snow blindness, in addition to hunger and exhaustion; many died during this part of the journey.

Xenophon and the surviving Ten Thousand marched northwestward toward the present-day city of Erzurum. Entering the territory of the warlike Chalybes they expected a hostile reception, but fortunately they encountered no difficulty. They arrived at the city of Gymnias, the center of a rich silver-mining district, where they learned they were not far from

Trapezus, which is the modern-day city of Trabzon on the Black Sea in Turkey. Xenophon wrote a famous passage about this part of the trip:

> When the men in front reached the summit and caught sight of the sea there was great shouting. Xenophon and the rearguard heard it and thought there were some more enemies attacking in front.... However, when the shouting got louder and drew nearer, and those who were constantly going forward started running towards the men in front who kept on shouting, and the more there were of them the more shouting there was, it looked then as there was something more serious. Xenophon galloped forward to the front with his cavalry. When he got near he heard what the cry was– The Sea! The Sea! Then they all began to run, the rearguard and all, and drove on the pack animals and horses at full speed; and when they had all got to the top, the soldiers, with tears in their eyes, embraced each other and their generals and captains.

Has sole command of army

Since Trapezus was a Greek colony, the soldiers were welcome even though the citizens were apprehensive about such a large, unruly band of men. At this point Xenophon thought of capturing a nearby native city and starting a new Greek colony. But the soldiers were not interested–they wanted only to get back home. The year was now 399 B.C., and they had been away from Greece for nearly two years. At this point Cheirosophus died, leaving Xenophon the sole leader of the Greek forces. In spite of the men's restlessness and their tendency to divide into smaller bands according to their native cities, he was able to keep the army together.

Xenophon led the Ten Thousand, who by now numbered only about 6,000, by land and sea to Chalcedon, which is now the city of Kadiköy, on the Asian shore opposite Byzantium. Xenophon had some difficulty in restraining his men from sacking the palace at Byzantium, which is now the Turkish capital of Istanbul. Since the soldiers were mercenaries who fought for money rather than patriotism, Xenophon was able to hire them out to Seuthes, the prince of Thrace, who used the Greeks to put down rebellious tribes. When Seuthes cheated the soldiers out of their pay, they were enlisted by the Spartans in a war with the Persians along the coasts of Asia Minor. This time the soldiers had better luck: they pillaged and sacked Persian towns, obtaining large amounts of plunder. By this time Xenophon had had enough of their unruly behavior; he turned the command over to an associate and returned to Athens.

Goes into exile in Sparta

Upon arriving in Athens, Xenophon found that his old master Socrates had died. The mood of the people had also changed and he no longer felt at home in his native city. At about this time Athens became an ally of the Persians against Sparta. Since Xenophon had long admired the disciplined, aristocratic life of the Spartans, he joined the Spartan cause. Fighting under the command of Agesilaus II in the Corinthian War, he participated in the defeat of the Athenians and Thebans at Coronea in central Greece in 394 B.C.

When Xenophon was banished from Athens because of his treachery, he went into exile in Sparta, where he was given a country estate at the town of Scillus near Mount Olympus. He stayed there for more than 20 years. During his exile he wrote the *Anabasis,* which has been called the world's first travelogue. He also wrote the *Greek History,* a continuation of the work by the historian Thucydides, which told the story of his native land from 411 B.C. to 362 B.C. It is the only surviving account of this important period in Greek history. Xenophon wrote extensively on the life of and teachings of Socrates as well as such subjects as horsemanship, hunting, military life, and the constitution of Sparta.

When Sparta suffered military reversals Xenophon lost his estate and retreated to the city of Corinth. In the meantime, Athens restored his citizenship, but it is thought he never returned. Xenophon died in Corinth sometime around the year 352 B.C. Although he was a brave and resourceful general, he is best remembered for his masterpiece, *Anabasis.*

Chuck Yeager

Born February 13, 1923,
Myra, West Virginia

C harles Elwood Yeager, known as Chuck, was born in Myra, West Virginia, on February 13, 1923. His father was a driller for natural gas in the West Virginia coalfields. As the United States began mobilizing for World War II, Yeager enlisted in the Army Air Force in September 1941, the summer after he graduated high school at the age of 18. In 1943 he became a flight officer, a noncommissioned officer who could pilot aircraft. During the last two years of the war he went to England, where he flew fighter missions into France and Germany.

Chuck Yeager, a test pilot for the United States Air Force, was the first person to fly a plane faster than the speed of sound.

Proves to be great fighter pilot

During his first eight missions, at the age of 20, Yeager shot down two German fighters. On his ninth mission he was shot down over German-occupied France. Suffering flak wounds, he bailed out of the airplane and was rescued by members of the French resistance, who smuggled him across the Pyrenees Mountains into Spain. After being jailed briefly in Spain he made his way back to England and flew fighter planes in support of the Allied invasion of Normandy.

On October 12, 1944, Yeager shot down five German fighter planes in succession. On November 6, flying a propeller-driven P-51 Mustang, he downed a Messerschmidt-262, one of Germany's new jet fighters, and damaged two more. On November 20 he shot down four FW-190s. By the end of the war, at the age of 22, Yeager was credited with having shot down 13½ German planes (he shared one victory with another pilot).

From 1946 to 1947 Yeager was trained as a test pilot at Wright Field in Dayton, Ohio, where he showed a talent for stunt-team flying. He was chosen to go to Muroc Field in California, later to become Edwards Air Force Base, to work on the top-secret *XS-1* project.

XS-1 project planned

At the end of the war, the U.S. Army had found that the Germans had developed both the world's first jet fighter and a rocket plane that had tested at speeds as fast as 596 miles an hour. Just after the war, Britain's *Gloster Meteor* had also raised the official world speed record to 606 miles per hour. The next record to be attained was to exceed the speed of sound, Mach 1, which was the goal of the *XS-1* project.

The measurement for the speed of sound was named after the German scientist Ernst Mach, who had discovered that sound travels at different speeds at different altitudes, temperatures, and wind speeds. For instance, on a calm day at 60°F at sea level the speed is about 760 miles an hour; this speed decreases at higher altitudes. Airplane pilots who had come close to the speed of sound in dives reported that their controls froze and the structure of the plane shook uncontrollably. A British test plane disintegrated as it approached the speed of sound. Because of these experiences, Mach 1 became known as the "sound barrier."

The army had developed an experimental plane called the *X-1* to break the barrier. Built by the Bell Aircraft Corporation, it was a rocket shaped like a bullet that was launched from another plane once it was airborne. The idea was to send up the *X-1* on a number of flights, each time getting a little closer to Mach 1. A top commercial test pilot had been making these flights and had reached .8 Mach, at which time the plane shook violently. The pilot demanded a large bonus to fly the plane up to Mach 1, but the army refused to pay the bonus. Yeager was given the job of piloting the *X-1* at his usual salary.

Yeager exceeds Mach 1

In his test flights Yeager was able to get the plane to fly at .9 Mach and still keep control. He believed the plane's heavy vibration would actually calm down after reaching Mach 1. The date of October 14, 1947, was set for breaking the sound barrier. On the night of October 12, Yeager went horseback riding and fell off his horse. The next day his right side was in pain. Afraid he would be replaced, Yeager visited a civilian doctor who told him he had broken two ribs.

Yeager kept his injury a secret. The broken ribs kept him from closing the plane's right side door, but he solved the problem by taking the handle of a broomstick with him and using it to close the door with his left hand. Early on the morning of October 14, Yeager went up in the B-29 bomber that carried the *X-1*. He entered the *X-1* and locked himself in at 7,000 feet. The B-29 released the *X-1* at 26,000 feet. At .87 Mach the violent vibrations began, but Yeager continued to push the aircraft faster. Just as he had predicted, at .96 Mach the aircraft steadied and he passed Mach 1. At that moment a giant roar–the first man-made sonic boom–was heard on the desert at the experimental test site. Yeager reached Mach 1.05 and stayed above Mach 1 for seven minutes. On his way back to the field he performed victory rolls and wing-over-wing stunts.

As soon as Yeager landed safely, the results were telephoned to the head of army aviation, who ordered the base not to give out any information about the flight. Rumors of the flight appeared in the aviation press in December 1947, but the air force–as the Army Air Force would become–did not confirm the successful test or release Yeager's name until June 1948.

Sets new record

Yeager continued to test planes at Edwards Air Force Base. In December 1953 he set a new record by flying the *X-1A* to Mach 2.4. After leaving Edwards in 1954 he went to Okinawa, Japan, where he flew Soviet planes captured in the Korean War to test their performance. He returned to the United States in 1957 to lead an air squadron; he flew on training operations and readiness maneuvers at Air Force bases in the United States and abroad. In 1961 he was appointed director of test flight operations at Edwards air force Base and the following year was made commandant of the Aerospace Research Pilot School at Edwards.

In 1963 Yeager tested the NF-104, an experimental plane designed for high altitude flying, to see if it could beat the record of 113,890 feet set by a Soviet military plane. Yeager had reached 108,000 feet when the plane spun out of control. He was forced to eject from the plane, severely burning the left side of his face and his left hand. He spent a month in the hospital but was able to return to his flying duties and his job as head of the experimental test pilot school.

Receives promotion

Yeager was promoted to brigadier general in 1969, by which time he had flown more than 100 missions in Southeast Asia in B-57 tactical bombers. He had become the most famous pilot in the United States, and the air force called upon him increasingly for its public relations and recruiting efforts. He served in a variety of air force positions until his retirement in 1975. He has received numerous military awards and was awarded the Presidential Medal of Freedom in 1985.

Yeager has written two autobiographies, *Yeager* and *Press On: Further Adventures of the Good Life*. In 1979 Tom Wolfe wrote a novel titled *The Right Stuff,* which retells the story of Yeager's *X-1* flights. A film by the same title was made in 1983, with the actor Sam Shepard playing the role of Yeager.

Chronology of Exploration

As an aid to the reader who wishes to trace the history of exploration or the explorers active in a particular location, the major expeditions within a geographical area are listed below in chronological order.

Africa: across the continent

1802-14	Pedro João Baptista and Amaro José
1854-56	David Livingstone
1858-64	David Livingstone
1872-73	David Livingstone
1873-77	Henry Morton Stanley
1877-80	Hermenegildo de Brito Capelo and Roberto Ivens
1884-85	Hermenegildo de Brito Capelo and Roberto Ivens
1888-90	Henry Morton Stanley
1896-98	Jean-Baptiste Marchand
1924-25	Delia Akeley

Africa: coast

1416-60	Henry the Navigator
1487-88	Bartolomeu Dias

Africa: east

1490-1526	Pero da Covilhã
1848	Johannes Rebmann
1848-49	Johann Ludwig Krapf
1848-49	Johannes Rebmann
1849	Johannes Rebmann
1851	Johann Ludwig Krapf
1857-59	Richard Burton and John Hanning Speke (with Sidi Mubarak Bombay)
1860-63	John Hanning Speke and James Augustus Grant (with Sidi Mubarak Bombay)
1862-64	Samuel White Baker and Florence Baker
1865-71	David Livingstone
1870-73	Samuel White Baker and Florence Baker

1871-73	Henry Morton Stanley (with Sidi Mubarak Bombay)
1883-84	Joseph Thomson
1905-06	Delia Akeley
1909-11	Delia Akeley

Africa: south

1849	David Livingstone
1850	David Livingstone
1851-52	David Livingstone

Africa: west

1352-53	Abu Abdallah Ibn Battutah
1795-99	Mungo Park
1805	Mungo Park
1827-28	René Caillié
1850-55	Heinrich Barth
1856-60	Paul Du Chaillu
1861-76	Friedrich Gerhard Rohlfs
1863	Paul Du Chaillu
1867	Paul Du Chaillu
1875-78	Pierre Savorgnan de Brazza
1879	Henry Morton Stanley
1879-81	Pierre Savorgnan de Brazza
1883-85	Pierre Savorgnan de Brazza
1891-92	Pierre Savorgnan de Brazza
1893	Mary Kingsley
1894	Mary Kingsley

Antarctica

1819-21	Fabian Gottlieb von Bellingshausen
1837-40	Jules-Sébastien-César Dumont d'Urville
1839-40	Charles Wilkes
1907-09	Ernest Shackleton

1910-12	Roald Amundsen
1914-16	Ernest Shackleton
1921-22	Ernest Shackleton
1928	Hubert Wilkins
1928-29	Richard Evelyn Byrd
1929	Hubert Wilkins
1933-34	Lincoln Ellsworth
1933-35	Richard Evelyn Byrd
1935-36	Lincoln Ellsworth
1937	Lincoln Ellsworth
1939-40	Richard Evelyn Byrd
1946-47	Richard Evelyn Byrd
1956	Richard Evelyn Byrd
1956-58	Vivian Fuchs
1989-90	Will Steger

Arabia

25 B.C	Aelius Gallus
1812-13	Hester Stanhhope
1854-55	Richard Burton
1877-78	Anne Blunt and Wilfrid Scawen Blunt
1879-80	Anne Blunt and Wilfrid Scawen Blunt
1913	Gertrude Bell

Arctic (*see also* North America: Northwest Passage)

1827	Edward Parry
1893-96	Fridtjof Nansen
1902	Robert Edwin Peary
1905-06	Robert Edwin Peary (with Matthew A. Henson)
1908-09	Robert Edwin Peary (with Matthew A. Henson)
1925	Roald Amundsen
1925	Richard Evelyn Byrd

1926	Roald Amundsen and Umberto Nobile
1926	Louise Arner Boyd
1926	Richard Evelyn Byrd
1926-27	Hubert Wilkins
1928	Louise Arner Boyd
1928	Hubert Wilkins
1931	Hubert Wilkins
1940	Louise Arner Boyd
1955	Louise Arner Boyd
1958	U.S.S. *Nautilus*
1986	Will Steger

Asia: interior

1866-68	Francis Garnier
1870-72	Nikolay Przhevalsky
1876	Nikolay Przhevalsky
1883-85	Nikolay Przhevalsky
1893-95	Sven Hedin
1895-97	Isabella Bird
1899	Fanny Bullock Workman
1899-1901	Sven Hedin
1900	Aurel Stein
1903-05	Sven Hedin
1906	Fanny Bullock Workman
1906-08	Aurel Stein
1913-15	Aurel Stein
1927-33	Sven Hedin
1934-36	Sven Hedin
1953	Edmund Hillary
1977	Edmund Hillary

Asia/Europe: link (see Europe/Asia: link)

Asia, south/China: link

| 629-45 B.C. | Hsüan-tsang |
| 138-26 B.C. | Chang Ch'ien |

1405-07	Cheng Ho
1407-09	Cheng Ho
1409-11	Cheng Ho
1413-15	Cheng Ho
1417-19	Cheng Ho
1421-22	Cheng Ho
1433-35	Cheng Ho

Australia

1605-06	Willem Janszoon
1642	Abel Tasman
1644	Abel Tasman
1770	James Cook
1798-99	Matthew Flinders
1801-02	Matthew Flinders
1801-02	Joseph Banks
1802-03	Matthew Flinders
1839	Edward John Eyre
1840-41	Edward John Eyre
1860-61	Robert O'Hara Burke and William John Wills

Aviation

1927	Charles Lindbergh
1928	Amelia Earhart
1930	Beryl Markham
1930	Amy Johnson
1931	Amy Johnson
1931	Wiley Post
1932	Amelia Earhart
1932	Amy Johnson
1933	Wiley Post
1935	Amelia Earhart
1936	Amelia Earhart
1936	Beryl Markham
1947	Chuck Yeager
1986	Dick Rutan and Jeana Yeager

Europe/Asia: link

454-43 B.C.	Herodotus
401-399 B.C.	Xenophon
334-23 B.C.	Alexander the Great
310-06 B.C.	Pytheas
1159-73	Benjamin of Tudela
1245-47	Giovanni da Pian del Carpini
1271-95	Marco Polo
1280-90	Rabban Bar Sauma
1487-90	Pero da Covilhã
1492-93	Christopher Columbus
1497-99	Vasco da Gama
1502-03	Vasco da Gama
1537-58	Fernão Mendes Pinto
1549-51	Saint Francis Xavier
1595-97	Cornelis de Houtman
1598-99	Cornelis de Houtman
1697-99	Vladimir Atlasov
1787	Jean François de Galaup, Comte de La Pérouse

Greenland

982	Erik the Red
1886	Robert Edwin Peary
1888	Fridtjof Nansen
1891-92	Robert Edwin Peary (with Matthew A. Henson)
1893-95	Robert Edwin Peary (with Matthew A. Henson)
1931	Louise Arner Boyd
1933	Louise Arner Boyd
1937	Louise Arner Boyd
1938	Louise Arner Boyd

Muslim World

915-17	Abu al-Hasan ʻAli al-Masʻudi
918-28	Abu al-Hasan ʻAli al-Masʻudi
943-73	Abu al-Kasim Ibn Ali al-Nasibi Ibn Hawkal
1325-49	Abu Abdallah Ibn Battutah

North America: coast

1001-02	Leif Eriksson
1493-96	Christopher Columbus
1497	John Cabot
1498	John Cabot
1502-04	Christopher Columbus
1508	Sebastian Cabot
1513	Juan Ponce de León
1513-14	Vasco Núñez de Balboa
1518-22	Hernán Cortés
1524	Giovanni da Verrazano
1534	Jacques Cartier
1534-36	Hernán Cortés
1535-36	Jacques Cartier
1539	Hernán Cortés
1541-42	Jacques Cartier
1542-43	João Rodrigues Cabrilho
1584	Walter Raleigh
1585-86	Walter Raleigh
1587-89	Walter Raleigh
1603	Samuel de Champlain
1604-07	Samuel de Champlain
1606-09	John Smith
1608-10	Samuel de Champlain
1609	Henry Hudson
1610	Samuel de Champlain
1614	John Smith
1792-94	George Vancouver

North America: Northwest Passage

1610-13	Henry Hudson
1776-79	James Cook
1819-20	Edward Parry

1821-23	Edward Parry
1824-25	Edward Parry
1845-47	John Franklin
1850-54	Robert McClure
1903-06	Roald Amundsen

North America: sub-Arctic

1654-56	Médard Chouart des Groselliers
1668	Médard Chouart des Groselliers
1668	Pierre Esprit Radisson
1670	Pierre Esprit Radisson
1679	Louis Jolliet
1682-83	Médard Chouart des Groselliers
1684	Pierre Esprit Radisson
1685-87	Pierre Esprit Radisson
1689	Louis Jolliet
1694	Louis Jolliet
1789	Alexander Mackenzie
1795	Aleksandr Baranov
1799	Aleksandr Baranov
1819-22	John Franklin
1825-27	John Franklin

North America: west

1527-36	Álvar Núñez Cabeza de Vaca (with Estevanico)
1538-43	Hernando de Soto
1539	Estevanico
1540-42	Francisco Vásquez de Coronado
1611-12	Samuel de Champlain
1613-15	Samuel de Champlain
1615-16	Samuel de Champlain
1615-16	Étienne Brulé

1621-23	Étienne Brulé
1657	Pierre Esprit Radisson
1659-60	Médard Chouart des Groselliers
1659-60	Pierre Esprit Radisson
1669-70	René-Robert Cavelier de La Salle
1672-74	Louis Jolliet
1678-83	René-Robert Cavelier de La Salle
1684-87	René-Robert Cavelier de La Salle
1769-71	Daniel Boone
1775	Daniel Boone
1792-94	Alexander Mackenzie
1792-97	David Thompson
1797-99	David Thompson
1800-02	David Thompson
1804-06	Meriwether Lewis and William Clark
1805-06	Zebulon Pike
1806-07	Zebulon Pike
1807-11	David Thompson
1811-13	Wilson Price Hunt and Robert Stuart
1823-25	Jedediah Smith
1824-25	Peter Skene Ogden
1825-26	Peter Skene Ogden
1826-27	Peter Skene Ogden
1826-28	Jedediah Smith
1828-29	Peter Skene Ogden
1829-30	Peter Skene Ogden
1842	John Charles Frémont
1843-44	John Charles Frémont
1845-48	John Charles Frémont
1848-49	John Charles Frémont
1850-51	Jim Beckwourth
1853-55	John Charles Frémont

Northeast Passage

1607	Henry Hudson
1918-20	Roald Amundsen
1931	Lincoln Ellsworth

North Pole (see Arctic)

Northwest Passage (see North America; Northwest Passage)

Oceans

1872-76	H.M.S. *Challenger*
1942-42	Jacques Cousteau
1948	August Piccard
1954	August Piccard
1960	Jacques Piccard
1968-80	*Glomar Challenger*
1969	Jacques Piccard

Pacific; south

1519-22	Ferdinand Magellan
1577-80	Francis Drake
1642-43	Abel Tasman
1721-22	Jacob Roggeveen
1766-68	Samuel Wallis
1766-69	Philip Carteret
1767-69	Louis-Antoine de Bougainville
1768-71	James Cook (with Joseph Banks)
1772-75	James Cook
1776-79	James Cook
1785-88	Jean François de Galaup, Comte de La Pérouse
1791	George Vancouver

1826-29	Jules-Sébastien-César Dumont d'Urville
1834-36	Charles Darwin
1838-39	Jules-Sébastien-César Dumont d'Urville
1838-42	Charles Wilkes
1930	Michael J. Leahy
1931	Michael J. Leahy
1932-33	Michael J. Leahy

South America; coast

1498-1500	Christopher Columbus
1499-1500	Alonso de Ojeda
1499-1500	Amerigo Vespucci
1501-1502	Amerigo Vespucci
1502	Alonso de Ojeda
1505	Alonso de Ojeda
1509-10	Alonso de Ojeda
1519-20	Ferdinand Magellan
1526-30	Sebastian Cabot
1527	Giovanni da Verrazano
1528	Giovanni da Verrazano
1594	Walter Raleigh
1595	Walter Raleigh
1617-18	Walter Raleigh
1831-34	Charles Darwin

South America; interior

1524-25	Francisco Pizarro
1526-27	Francisco Pizarro
1531-41	Francisco Pizarro
1540-44	Álvar Núñez Cabeza de Vaca
1541-42	Francisco de Orellana
1769-70	Isabel Godin des Odonais
1799-1803	Alexander von Humboldt
1903	Annie Smith Peck
1904	Annie Smith Peck
1908	Annie Smith Peck

1911	Hiram Bingham
1912	Hiram Bingham
1915	Hiram Bingham

Space

1957	*Sputnik*
1958-70	*Explorer 1*
1959-72	*Luna*
1961	Yury Gagarin
1962	John Glenn
1962-75	*Mariner*
1963	Valentina Tereshkova
1967-72	*Apollo*
1969	Neil Armstrong
1975-83	*Viking*
1977-90	*Voyager 1* and *2*
1983	Sally Ride
1990-	Hubble Space Telescope

Tibet

1624-30	Antonio de Andrade
1811-12	Thomas Manning
1865-66	Nain Singh
1867-68	Nain Singh
1879-80	Nikolay Przhevalsky
1892-93	Annie Royle Taylor
1898	Susie Carson Rijnhart
1901	Sven Hedin
1915-16	Alexandra David-Neel
1923-24	Alexandra David-Neel

Explorers by Country of Birth

*If an expedition were sponsored by a country other than the explorer's place of birth,
the sponsoring country is listed in parentheses after the explorer's name.*

Angola

Pedro João Baptista (Portugal)
Amaro José

Australia

Michael J. Leahy
Hubert Wilkins

Canada

Louis Jolliet
Peter Skene Ogden
Susie Carson Rijnhart

China

Rabban Bar Sauma
Chang Ch'ien

Cheng Ho
Hsüan-tsang

Ecuador

Isabel Godin des Odonais

England

Samuel White Baker
Joseph Banks
Gertrude Bell
Isabella Bird
Anne Blunt
Wilfrid Scawen Blunt
Richard Burton
Philip Carteret
H.M.S. *Challenger*

James Cook
Charles Darwin
Francis Drake
Edward John Eyre
Matthew Flinders
John Franklin
Vivian Fuchs
Henry Hudson (Netherlands)
Amy Johnson
Mary Kingsley
Thomas Manning
Beryl Markham (Kenya)
Edward Parry
Walter Raleigh
John Smith
John Hanning Speke
Hester Stanhope
Annie Royle Taylor
David Thompson
George Vancouver
Samuel Wallis
William John Wills (Australia)

Estonia

Fabian Gottlieb von Bellingshausen (Russia)

France

Louis-Antoine de Bougainville
Étienne Brulé
René Caillié
Jacques Cartier
Samuel de Champlain
Médard Chouart des Groselliers
Paul Du Chaillu (United States)
Jacques Cousteau
Alexandra David-Neel
Jules-Sébastien-César Dumont d'Urville
Francis Garnier

Jean François de Galaup, Comte de La Pérouse
René-Robert Cavelier de La Salle
Jean-Baptiste Marchand
Pierre Esprit Radisson

Germany

Heinrich Barth (Great Britain)
Alexander von Humboldt
Johann Ludwig Krapf
Johannes Rebmann
Friedrich Gerhard Rohlfs

Greece

Herodotus
Pytheas
Xenophon

Hungary

Aurel Stein (Great Britain)

Iceland

Leif Eriksson

India

Nain Singh

Iraq

Abu al-Kasim Ibn Ali al-Nasibi Ibn Hawkal
Abu al-Hasan `Ali al-Mas`udi

Ireland

Robert O'Hara Burke (Australia)
Robert McClure
Ernest Shackleton

Italy

Pierre Savorgnan de Brazza (France)
John Cabot (Great Britain)
Sebastian Cabot (England, Spain)
Giovanni da Pian del Carpini
Christopher Columbus (Spain)
Marco Polo
Giovanni da Verrazano (France)
Amerigo Vespucci (Spain, Portugal)

Macedonia

Alexander the Great

Morocco

Abu Abdallah Ibn Battutah
Estevanico

Netherlands

Cornelis de Houtman
Willem Janszoon
Jacob Roggeveen
Abel Tasman

New Zealand

Edmund Hillary

Norway

Roald Amundsen
Erik the Red (Iceland)
Fridtjof Nansen

Nyasaland

Sidi Mubarak Bombay (Great Britain)
James Chuma (Great Britain)

Portugal

Antonio de Andrade
Hermenegildo de Brito Capelo
João Rodrigues Cabrilho (Spain)
Pero da Covilhã
Bartolomeu Dias
Vasco da Gama
Henry the Navigator
Roberto Ivens
Ferdinand Magellan (Spain)
Fernão Mendes Pinto

Romania

Florence Baker

Rome

Aelius Gallus

Russia

(*see also* Union of Soviet Socialist Republics)

Vladimir Atlasov
Aleksandr Baranov
Nikolay Przhevalsky

Scotland

David Livingstone
Alexander Mackenzie
Mungo Park
Robert Stuart (United States)
Joseph Thomson

Spain

Benjamin of Tudela
Álvar Núñez Cabeza de Vaca

Francisco Vásquez de Coronado
Hernán Cortés
Vasco Núñez de Balboa
Alonso de Ojeda
Francisco de Orellana
Francisco Pizarro
Juan Ponce de León
Hernando de Soto
Saint Francis Xavier

Sweden

Sven Hedin

Switzerland

Auguste Piccard
Jacques Piccard

Union of Soviet Socialist Republics

Yury Gagarin
Luna
Sputnik
Valentina Tereshkova

United States of America

Delia Akeley
Apollo
Neil Armstrong
Jim Beckwourth
Hiram Bingham
Daniel Boone
Louise Arner Boyd
Richard Evelyn Byrd
William Clark
Amelia Earhart

Lincoln Ellsworth
Explorer 1
John Charles Frémont
John Glenn
Glomar Challenger
Matthew A. Henson
Hubble Space Telescope
Wilson Price Hunt
Meriwether Lewis
Charles Lindbergh
Mariner
U.S.S. *Nautilus*
Robert Edwin Peary
Annie Smith Peck
Zebulon Pike
Wiley Post
Sally Ride
Dick Rutan
Jedediah Smith
Will Steger
Viking
Voyager 1 and *2*
Charles Wilkes
Fanny Bullock Workman
Chuck Yeager
Jeana Yeager

Wales

Henry Morton Stanley (United States)

Index

Bold denotes figures profiled

Cheirosophus 868-869
Chen Tsu-i 222
Cheng Ho 221-224
Ch'eng-tu 460
Cherokee 118, 119
Chesapeake Bay 142, 470, 764-765
Cheyenne 85
Cheyenne Peak 663
Chiaha 770
Chibcha 479
Chickahominy River 764
Chickasaw (tribe) 770
Chihuahua, Mexico 348, 663
Childersburg, Alabama 770
Children's Crusade 96
Chile 510, 732, 834
Chillicothe, Ohio 120
Chiloe Island 300
Chimbu Valley 521
Chin-liu, China 460
China 461, 463, 469, 484, 509-
    510, 513, 687, 691-692, 814
China Inland Mission 814
Chinese Turkistan 461
Chira River 672
Chitambo 554
Chobe River 547-548
Choctaw Bluff, Alabama 770
Cholon (Saigon, Vietnam) 394
Cholula, Mexico 278
Cho Oyu 450
Choqquequirau, Peru 99
**Chouart des Groseilliers,
    Médard 225-230**
Christian, Fletcher 189
Christmas Island 265
Chryse Planitia 845
Ch'üan-chou, China 79
Chu Chan-chi 223
Chukchi Peninsula 62
Chukchi Sea 611
Chuma, James 116, **231-237,**
    552, 554, 826
Churchill River 561
Churchill, Winston 748
Church Missionary Society 503,
    505
Church of England 316
Church of Vidigueira 392
Chu Ti, Prince 222

Cilicia, Turkey 88
Cimarron River 761
Ciudad Bolivar 479
Clapperton, Hugh 72, 637
Clark, George Rogers 119,
    529
Clark, William 485, 528-537
Clearwater River 534
Cleopatris, Egypt 384
Cleveland, Ohio 702
Clinch River 118
Clinch River valley 119
Clitus 9
*The Coast of Northeast Green-
    land* 132
Coats Land 748
Cochin, China 394, 397
Cocos Islands 302
Coelho, Nicolau 387
Cofitachequi 769
Coiba 615
Collins, Michael 29, 37
Collinson, Richard 17, 368, 600,
    602
Colombia 479, 615, 625
Colorado River 166, 270-271,
    530, 621, 759-760
Columbia 37, 38, 725, 832
Columbia River 372, 483-484,
    530, 534-535, 621-622, 821,
    824, 832
Columbia River valley 824
Columbus, Bartholomew 239,
    241, 249, 251-252
Columbus, Christopher 169-170,
    238-254, 275, 288, 313, 386,
    487, 614, 623, 695, 796, 839
Columbus, Diego 238, 240, 251,
    254, 696
Columbus, Ferdinand 239, 241,
    252
Comanche 761
Comogre 616
Compagnie du Nord 229
Compagnie van Verre 455
Company of One Hundred Asso-
    ciates 217
Compostela, Mexico 270
Concepción, Chile 300
Concepción 567, 571

D

Dahar-June 787
Dahe, Qin 803
Daily Mail 492
Dakar, Senegal 426
Dalai Lama 307-309, 575-577, 753
The Dalles, Oregon 621
Damascus, Syria 76, 88, 97, 109, 157, 597
Damietta, Egypt 97
Danube River 44
Dardanelles 6
Darién 616
Darien Peninsula 625, 670
Darius I (of Persia) 434
Darius II (of Persia) 867
Darius III (of Persia) 7, 8
Darling River 145, 147
Darling, William 357
Dartmouth, England 472
Darwin, Australia 491-492
Darwin, Charles 292-305, 474
Darwin, Erasmus 292
David, Edgeworth 747
David-Neel, Alexandra 306-310
Davis, John 458
Davis Strait 472, 525
De Long, George Washington 606
Dead Sea 597
Dean Channel 564
Deccan, India 596
Deena 633
Deep Sea Drilling Project 406
Defoe, Daniel
Deganawidah 215
Deimos 587
Delaware Bay 470
Delaware River 470
Delft 487
Delhi, India 23
Denbei 42
Denver, Colorado 84
Derb-el-Haj 76
Derendingen 502
Descartes Mountains 32
A Description of New England 765

Desideri, Ippolito 576
de Soto, Hernando (see **Soto, Hernando de**)
Detroit Arctic Expedition 857
Detroit, Michigan 120, 485, 538
Devil's Ballroom 20
Devon Island 16
Dias, Bartolomeu 241, 288, **311-314,** 386, 388, 426
Dias, Dinis 426
Días, Melchor 270, 271
Dickson, James 633, 635
Diderot, Denis 127
Diebetsch, Josephine 645
Diemen, Anthony van 810
Dieppe, France 837
Dietrich, Rosine 504
Digges Island 473
Dione, moon 849
Discoverie of Guiana 715
Discovery 264-266, 464, 472-473, 830-833
District of Orleans 536
Diyarbakir 77
Djakarta, Indonesia 127, 190
Djenné, Mali 180, 579
Djibouti 580, 583-584
Dnieper River 41
Dolak Island 487
Dolphin 188, 190, 191, 257
Dominican Republic 615
Donnacona 194, 195
Donn River 41
Dorantes, Andres 165-166, 347-348
Doudart de Lagrée, Ernest 396
Drake, Francis 315-320
Druid 296
Druses 786-787
Druze 87
Dry Tortugas 697
Dubois River 530
Du Chaillu, Paul 321-324
Dudh Kosi River 752
Duifken 486-487
Duke, Charles 32
Duluth, Minnesota 142, 823
Dumont d'Urville, Jules-Sébastien-César 325-329, 511, 853

L

Mercury 481, 587-588, 850
Mercury 31, 401
Mercury 5 28
"Mercury Seven" 401, 404
Mercy Bay 602-603
Méré 582
Meru 3
Meryon, Charles 784-785, 787
Mesawa 503
Mesopotamia 8, 87, 97, 219-220, 808
Messina, Sicily 97
Mestiza 479
Metternich, Clemens von 475
Metzenbaum, Howard 405
Mexico City, Mexico 167, 270, 272, 273, 541
Michilimackinac 216, 496, 516
Micronesia 327
Midjökull 342
Miletus 6
Mill, John Stuart 358
Minab River 10
Mindanao Island 571
Minnetaree (tribe) 532, 534
Mirambo 790
Miranda 850
Mirnyi 91-92
Miss Boyd Land 131
Mission San Gabriel 760
Mississippi River 165, 494, 496-497, 513-518, 529-530, 661-662, 767, 770, 823
Mississippi Valley 517
Missoula, Montana 620
Missouri 483, 533, 662
Missouri River 483, 496, 516, 530-533, 535-536, 759, 823
Missouri (tribe) 531
Mitchell, Edgar 31
Mocha, Yemen 666
Moffat, Robert 544
Mogadishu, Somalia 223
Mohawk (tribe) 215, 225
Mohi, Hungary 184
Mojave Desert 760
Mojave River 760
Mojave (tribe) 621, 760
Mîle St. Nicolas, Haiti 245
Mollison, Jim 492, 493, 592

Moluccas (Spice Islands) 127, 174, 318, 457, 567, 570-571, 573, 733, 865
Mombasa, Kenya 3, 113, 223, 289, 389, 504, 718, 828
Möngkhe 184
Mongol Empire 688
Mongolia 704-705
Mongolia and the Tangut Country 706
Mongols 65-67, 77, 97, 183, 185, 576, 687, 691-693
Moniz, Felipa Perestrello de 238
Montana 484, 533
Monterey, California 83, 510, 761, 834
Montevideo, Uruguay 296, 299
Montezuma 274-276, 278, 279
Montgomerie, Thomas George 751
Monticello 482
Montpelier, France 95
Montreal, Quebec, Canada 195, 226, 483-484, 497, 512-513, 516, 518
Monts, Pierre de 214
Moore, John 784
Moors 241-242, 424
Morant Bay 357
Morel, Edmund 136
Moriussaw, Greenland 432
Morocco 106, 287, 736, 763, 861
Morovejo, Evaristo 100-101
Morozko, Luka 41
Morrow, Ann 541
Moscoso, Luis de 771
Moscow, Russia 184, 701, 703
Mossel Bay 312, 388
Mount Aconcagua 99, 101, 654
Mountain Green 620
Mountain men 758
Mountains of the Moon 798
Mount Albert 506
Mount Ararat 689
Mount Brown 361
Mount Cameroon 500
Mount Chimborazo 480
Mount Cook 450
Mount Desert Island 214
Mount Egmont 450

South China Sea 222
Southern Alps 449-450
South Georgia Island 91, 749
South Island, New Zealand 259, 263, 327, 449, 810-811
South Magnetic Pole 328, 747
South Orkney Islands 328
South Pass, Wyoming 372, 485, 757
South Peak 451
South Pole 14, 18-20, 158, 160-161, 163, 338, 377, 452-453, 744, 746-747, 804, 859
South Seas 509, 513
South Shetland Islands 92, 93, 328
Soviet Space Commission 818
Soyuz 1 382
Space Telescope Science Institute (Baltimore, Maryland) 466
Spanish-American War 158
Spanish Armada 315, 319-320, 714
Spanish Inquisition 241
Spanish Trail 372
Sparta 870
Speke, John Hanning 45-46, 112, 113-114, 153-156, 502, 551, 580, 722, **772-777,** 794
Spencer Gulf 355, 356, 361, 362
Spencer, Herbert 358
Spice Islands 127, 174, 318, 457, 567, 570-571, 573, 733, 865
Spirit of St. Louis 539, 542
Spitsbergen Islands 130, 160, 642
Spitsbergen, Norway 21, 22, 337, 365, 611-612, 858
Spruce, Richard 481
Sputnik 26, 36, 351, 353, 379, 555, 557, **778-782**
Sri Lanka 44, 51, 79, 222-223, 596, 598, 693, 862
Srinigar, India 105, 406
Stadacona (Quebec City, Quebec) 195-196
Stafford, Thomas 29
Stag Lane 489
Stalin, Joseph 779
Stanhope, Hester 783-787
Stanislaus River 760
Stanley Falls 795

Stanley, Henry Morton 115, 134-135, 138, 233, 236, 553, **788-799,** 828
Stanley Pool 134-135, 795
St. Ann's Bay 253
Station Camp Creek, Kentucky 118
St. Augustine, Florida 319, 696
St. Croix, Virgin Islands 248
Stefansson, Vilhjalmur 857
Steger International Polar Expedition 802
Steger, Will 800-805
Stein, Aurel 806-808
Stephen of Cloyes 96
Stewart, James 542
St. Helena 302, 834
St. Ignace 496
Stingray Point 764
St. John's, Newfoundland 196
St. Joseph, Missouri 483
St. Lawrence River 193, 195, 212-213, 215, 227, 255, 497-498, 526
St. Louis, MIssouri 483-485, 530-531, 536, 539-540, 662
Stockton, Robert F. 373
St. Paul, Minnesota 662
St. Petersburg, Russia 420, 705, 708
Strabo 384
Strait of Belle Isle 194, 526
Strait of Georgia 833
Strait of Gibraltar 408, 415, 710
Strait of Hormuz 223
Strait of Juan de Fuca 832, 854
Strait of Magellan 124, 174, 188, 300, 318-319, 327, 458, 569, 600
Straits of Mackinac 514
Straits of Malacca 459
Streaky Bay 356
Stuart, John McDouall 144, 146, 149
Stuart, Robert 483-485
St. Vincent, West Indies 357
Submarine Force Museum 613
Sué River 582
Suffren 394
Sulpicians 513